A GUIDE TO NAVIGATING YOUR INHERITED HOME SALE

All The Steps to Selling Your Inherited Home

DR. SONATTACAMARA

Table Of Contents

Part One: Legal Aspects Of Inherited Homes

CHAPTER 1
DEALING WITH INHERITED HOMES:
BEST PRACTICE FOR FAMILIES

D ealing with the inherited home is a tricky subject since there could be several complicated issues to solve. It is not uncommon for the person selling an inherited home to have a sentimental attachment to the property, which makes selling it an emotionally overwhelming decision.

However, making the decision to selling it could mean an amicable settlement of the property from several angles. While deciding to sell it could be the best idea to address all the complications, some proven tips can help homeowners approach the issue in a meticulous manner, with fewer problems and satisfactory results for all the stakeholders concerned.

Here we will discuss the different aspects of splitting the property with family members and the best practices involved.

Benefits of Selling

There are several benefits to selling the inherited property. In some cases, along with the inherited property, the heirs end up inheriting a lot of unexpected difficulties, commitments, legal and financial implications as well.

No matter if you are a single heir or one of multiple heirs to the property, selling it as quickly as you can is a way to save a great amount of money, time, stress, and the tiring effort involved in the settlement process. Every situation when someone inherits a home typically different from each other.

The traditional means of selling homes is a good option if you find that there are no outstanding mortgages and the property is in good shape, where it does not require any repairs or cleaning to sell it. If you can easily afford any necessary repairs and cleaning, while handling the selling process, then you can choose the usual ways of selling it.

When there are siblings or family members who share the property with you as legal heirs, there might be some disagreement about how the settlement should occur. Therefore, selling the property could save you hassles. Once you convert it to money, the money can be distributed among the heirs. One concern that you need to address is the amount of time required to sell the property, since it is uncertain when it may sell.

If the house is underwater, meaning that the worth of owning it is less than what it is owed on it, it is recommended that you sell it as quickly as possible. A short sale of the home can come to your aid if there are mortgage payments due which you are not willing or unable to pay. If one or more heirs inheriting the property have an urgent need for cash, then a quick home sale is an option.

Sometimes, you might have some added tax benefits in selling the home. At times, you might also feel that you just want to get rid of the burden by selling it quickly, in order to get on with your life as smoothly as possible.

If the property is located in another city or state, assuming the responsibilities of maintaining a vacant house can be real burden that you may not be prepared to endure. If the house goes to probate, then even if there are no residents, the property must be maintained.

The property taxes, insurance premiums, utilities, homeowner association fees and other costs to maintain must be carried on by someone. Depending how long the probate period lasts, families need to pay for maintenance of the home, as long with the legal and other fees connected to owning and selling the property.

Also at the end of the probate, you will have to once again incur the hassles and expenditure of repairing and selling the home. Under each conditions, if you benefits is lower than your hassles and commitments, it is advisable you sell the home to investors.

Looking at several angles, selling an inherited home appears to be the best answer to the problems associated with inheritance.

Dealing with Family Members

Disputes among the siblings or legal heirs over the settlement of the inherited property are very common. Often, disputes over a property are dominated by some past issues of sibling rivalry and are a fight for dominance. During the absence of parental guidance, adult siblings are left to face the scenario of ambiguity or disagreement over their rightful rule.

Ensure that disputes and disagreements do not lead to litigation since this will worsen the situation, cause issues with family members, create uncertainty waiting for the issues to be legally settled and hassles associated with legally settled and hassles associated with legal hearings. The tremendous cost involved in litigation is certainly a wasteful expenditure. Litigation can hardly heal the differences.

The situation can be avoided. There is always a solution that can be made for a peaceful settlement so that creative solutions to these problem can be facilitated, and there is a mutual gain for all the concerned.

The good solutions is for one of the heirs to buy the property from the others. If you inherit the home with your siblings, the rule is that it is even split unless otherwise stated in the will. If one of the siblings is interested in keeping it while the other wants sell it off, then the siblings interested can buy the property.

The cost involved in this process is minimal and includes the appraiser's fees and the closing costs. If this will work, then you just have to pay your siblings in cash for his share and get the title of the property transferred into your sole name through a deed. A private agreement can prove useful under some normal circumstances.

If you or your sibling cannot qualify for a mortgage, the one who does not wish to keep the house can finance the transaction. This will mean you will not need a house loan or incur out of pocket expenses.

For the private agreement, all that you need to do is to make a promissory note to your sibling for his or her share of the value as per the appraisal. The amount due to him or her can be paid in monthly installments along with interest. With this arrangement, you can buy out the property in time. If necessary, you may also make a deed of trust that gives him the power to foreclose if you default on payments.

Selling or renting the property could be the solution if none of the siblings are interested in keeping the property. If you have a friendly relationship, meaning that you can get along for a long time period as co-owner of the property, you can rent out the property and take your due share out of the proceeds monthly.

If one of the siblings manages the collection of rental payments, then the effort can be rewarded by the other with a little increase in the share. Whatever the terms are, it is good to record them in a written agreement. However, the best arrangement under these circumstances could be to sell the property, subtract the expenses, costs involved and the commissions paid and then divide the resulting amount among you.

Selling the property as soon as you inherit also helps you save on the capital gains tax. Capital gains tax for sale of the inherited property is calculated on the property value after the death of the decedent.

Since the difference may not be much if the time period is short, then you may be left with nothing to pay in capital gains tax. A lawsuit for partition should be the last option for you to settle the inherited property if you cannot come into an amicable agreement with your sibling over the settlement.

Filing a lawsuit can ask the judge to order the sale of your home and you can terminate your co-ownership. This is complicated process and the judge usually appoints a mediator first, to get the property ready for sale.

If you are at odds with each other, you and your sibling may not be able to do this. Therefore, you have to have an agent to sell the home and mediate between you both and you both need to be prepared for this.

Holdovers Living in Estate

While inheriting the property, you must also address the issue of holdover living in estate. If one of your siblings or yourself is living in the property, you need to come to an agreement with all the heirs whether the concerned individual will continue to live there or vacate.

In case of continuing to live there, the terms be clearly drafted out. If the right to remain there is mentioned in the will, then it cannot be challenged. If it has to be challenged for some reason, the necessary legal proceedings must be adhered to.If the decision is made to sell the property, then the property must be vacated in a definite timeline facilitating the sale. If the occupant wishes to continue residing in the property despite the sale, then it must be dealt with accordingly.

If you are inheriting a property with tenants living in it, you must fulfill some responsibilities from the position of a Landlord. If the property is sold, the legal rights of the tenants must be given due consideration. For complicated situations like this, it is always good to consult competent attorney.

Splitting Up Items Inside

Any decision pertaining to the settlement of the property or its contents among the legal heirs must follow the guidance given in the will. Sentimental objects are invaluable and settling them must happen out of the legal conventions in manual agreement between the siblings.

In case there is no will enacted by the owner of the property, then the state's laws regarding intestate accession will come into play. Depending on whether the will or the law requires the estate to be divided equally, the heirs must act accordingly.

A few problem will arise, regarding the value of the estate and how it will be split up. However, since the value of sentimental objects are often subjective and cannot be decided by an appraiser, the real challenge would ease if the different siblings wish to claim a particular item for themselves. In this case, the right solution would be to auction the personal items and distribute the sale value among the siblings equally.

A real estate agent can be appointed to decide the value of the property. The challenge here may be how to divide the real estate among the heirs in an acceptable way.

The two approaches that the siblings could take include either selling the property to divide the proceeds or to keep the property and share the use. If the estate also features assets that cannot be distributed pro-rata basis, an equal division of value is the solution.

If a sibling wants to hold the property, then the others can get the cash equal to their share of the property or other assets as it may be decided. Ultimately, everyone involved in the deal walks away with his or her share of the property in the right proportion.Dealing with the leftover items in the estate could be a laborious task and a bothersome job while attempting to settle a property.In this situation, you might need to categorize the items as those to keep, those to sell, those to donate and those to throw away.

Remember that during an estate sale, people may be ready to buy even the oddest things. Therefore, make some effort to see that as many things as possible are sold or auctioned away to be converted into cash and distributed among the heirs.

CHAPTER 2
LEGAL ASPECTS OF SELLING AN INHERITED HOME

While selling an inherited home is the one good and viable solution to effectively address the complications and disputes connected to splitting the property, there are a few legal aspects you first must know so that you are able to make informed decisions and avoid some complications that may rice.

Will

A will on an inherited estate is a legally written document that is authoritative in deciding what should happen to the property regarding the voluntary decisions of the estate owner. The author of a will is usually the sole owner of the property who enjoys complete rights to it and who drafts the will in favor of the legal heirs or the individual(s) he or she wants to inherit the property.

The will also nominate an executor who has complete authority to oversee the proceedings of the inheritance and ensure that the transfer of titles happen as stated in the will. The will concerning the estate makes the process of inheritance undisputable, smooth and hassle free. If there is no will in place, then the established legal laws that govern the given state will come into play and, if needed, a court will intervene to settle any issues.

The inheritance gifted with a will can happen through three ways. The most common method is called a Solemn Form Probate. Upon the appointment of the executor, he or she sends out a notice to all the heirs at law which becomes legally binding.

Heirs at law are those who inherit the estate in the absence of a lawful will. However, they might or might not be the beneficiaries as per the will. The notice requires all the heirs in to either object or contest the will if they wish to before the mentioned deadline.

The petition should be accompanied by the original will. The proof of executing the will needs to be furnished, either through self-proving affidavit or testimonies of witnesses. The court will appoint someone to act as *guardian ad litem* for any minors or incapacitated individuals inheriting the property.

The second method is a Common Form Probate. This procedure can be carried out without any notice to the heirs in law, but cannot be deemed as binding for four years following the appointment of the executor or four years after the minor heir attains the legal age of inheritance.

The proof of proper execution and the need to provide the original will are the same in this case as in the case of Solemn Probate. Following Common Form Probate, heirs on law or other interested parties can file an objection anytime up to four years after the Common Form Probate.The executor can be selected by the majority of the beneficiaries. For the sake of minors or incapacitated heirs, the courts appoint a *guardian ad litem*. Probate is not required when there is no property to be divided under the terms of the will and testamentary letters are not necessary to take the control of the assets.

But it is essential to file the will of the deceased with the probate court. Unlike bank accounts, real estate properties will not automatically pass on to the co-owner who survives. To transfer the title of an automobile, probate is not needed.

In the absence of a will that names an executor, state law gives out a list of people who can discharge the responsibility. If there is a necessity for a probate court proceeding, then the court will choose the administrator based on the priority list. The laws vary between states as to what happens to a deceased person's property who dies without enacting a valid will.

If the deceased person was married, the surviving spouse will get the largest share of the estate. In cases where there were no children, the surviving spouse inherits the entirety of the property. The laws of every state direct how the children inherit the property.

Taxes

Inheritance is not always a happy thing that happens smoothly. Often there are a lot of confusion and frustration associated with it. While the authors of the will pass on the property with the best of intentions, inheritors often have to spend a great deal of money, effort and time.The tax burdens accompanying the inherited property are always a matter of concern and confusion. When inheriting a home, you need to know what kinds of taxes are attached to the home and what your obligations are. Tax laws also significantly differ from state.

Therefore, you need to understand the inheritance tax laws of your state. For simplicity, the broad kinds of taxes applicable over inheritance are discussed here.

Estate Tax: Federal estate tax does not apply to inheritance since there have been changes made through legal statutes.However, there is an upper limit regarding the property value which estate taxes would apply. Certain states, however, impose their own taxes on inherited assets.

Inheritance Tax: There is not a federal inheritance tax.

While it is common for some people to refer to the federal estate tax as inheritance tax or a death tax, there is a huge difference between these two types of taxes.

In some states, both of these types of taxes do apply. It is the responsibility of the estate to pay estate taxes and not the heirs. On the other hand, the heirs pay the inheritance tax.

The tax you are required to pay depends on where you live and what laws govern the state.

Property Tax: Upon inheriting the property, the heirs are required to pay property taxes.

Property taxes must be paid for as long as heirs continue to own the property. Usually you will be required to pay more taxes than those paid the original owner because property tax value will be decided by the current value of the property based on a reassessment.

In some states, the reassessment is not done if the heir is the spouse or child of the owner passing on the property.

Capital Gains Tax: Capital Gains taxes are applicable when you decide to sell your inherited home for the fair market value or more.

This means that you will have to pay the taxes on the profit margin you have from the sale of the property. This is assessed on how much you sell the property for and what the value of the property was when value has not gone up.

Reporting the Inheritance: It is necessary for the executor of the estate to report the inherited property by filing an estate tax return.

The basis of the inherited home is decided on whether the sale is a gain or loss. It is decided based on when you inherited the property. In most cases, the basis for inherited home is the market value of the property on the date when the deceased person died.

Reporting the Sale: While selling the inherited home, you are expected to report the sales on your income taxes.

Subtract the amount you received from the sale from the base amount to calculate whether you gained or lost from the deal and report it on the IRS Schedule D. you will also need to copy the gain or loss amount over to your 1040 tax return form.

Name on Property

When you inherit the personal property, the process is very simple and the procedure is straightforward. The will or the court's decision may be enough to transfer the title of the property to you. In case of inheriting real estate, things can be a bit more complicated.

This is because the ownership of the property must be modified to state that you are the new owner. Generally, in this case, the executor of the will or the administrator nominated by the probate court will issue a new deed that names you as the new owner of the property.

The documents you will need in this regard include the death certificates of all the owner and the probated will of previous owner, if available. You must consult the original deed of the property to confirm that the property was not owned jointly during the time of death of the deceased.

If the property is owned jointly, then the surviving owner inherits the property in full. Therefore, you will have to confirm whether you can inherit it by reading the death certificate and determining the order of the joint owner's death.

If the person that you inherit the property from has died first, then the property would revert back to the other owner and so you must now establish your claim as the legal heir to the property. If the will states you as the inheritor, then you will require an executor's deed.

If the inheritance is facilitated lawfully by the court in the absence of the will, then you must present an administrator's deed. Both kinds of deeds must describe the property legally and mention your name as the new owner. Along with the administrator who issued the deed, you need to sign the new deed in the presence of a notary public. If needed, you also be able to produce a copy of the probated will as part of making the deed.

Living Estates

A life estate means someone having a real property interest for lifetime, which will automatically revert back to the owner, his family, or an authorized third party. It is a kind of possessory interest entitling the tenant to benefit from the property. The one receiving the remainder of the life estate is known as the "remainderman".

There are two types of life estates: the standard life estate and life estate *purautre vie*. An estate is said to be purautre vie, when a lease is made of lands or tenements to a man, to hold for the life of another person.

The standard life estate lasts as longas the person occupying the property is alive. While the life estate *purautre vie* is based on the life of a third person.

The objective of both life estate types is to give the rights over the property to the beneficiary for the duration of a single life and then returning the property back to the original owner, his family, or an authorized third party.

Creating a life is done by redrafting the property's deed to mention that it is a life estate with the remainder passing in fee to somebody else. Like any other property transfer, both parties must sign this deed, have it notarized and then submitted it to the recording office of the state.

Since living trusts have come to replace the role played by life estates, they are not commonly used today. However, there are some great advantages to this archaic form of inheritance.

This method is highly useful to the legal heirs to increase the property value following the death of the decedent. A life estate can also help avoid probate which is a legally required process to transfer the property from the deceased to his descendants.

In other words, a life estate can be called "instant transfer". There are also some significant tax implications in using a life estate. Section 2036 of the Federal Estate Tax Code treats life estates as a gift. The gift tax must only be paid if the value exceeds the specified amount.

If the property is sold after the end of a life estate, there is no net gain that needs to be reported on taxes on account of the value step-up. In case your local property is located in a different country or state, you need to take a cautious approach while drafting a life estate by using the services of as attorney.

Some countries do not recognize living estates. In these case, a skilled and experienced lawyer will have some better options to help you avoid the burdening tax costs.

CHAPTER 3
VACATING AN INHERITED HOME

I f you think the home vacating process after inheriting a home is stressful, then don't plan for your move and watch how much more stressful it will become. Of course, the simplest piece of advice if you are planning on vacating a home, would be to sit down with someone who has recently relocated and quiz them about their experiences.

Taking these experiences and learning from their mistakes will help you to plan your move effectively. If you don't have someone in this position that you can talk to, then this chapter will at least highlight some area that you might want to look at and to use them as the basis for your own moving plan.

A common mistake people make is to pack all of their important documents in boxes and then transporting them with everything else that is being moved. Once they reach their destination, they have problems when information is needed and cannot be found because it isn't immediately at hand. So, before you pack these items, take the time to write down all of your account numbers (bank, mortgage, insurance, etc.) and contact details onto a piece of paper and carry it with you to your new home, rather than in the transportation vehicle.

A better idea is to photocopy all of the important documents and keep those with you all the times. Then you could ask a trusted family member or friend to hold of it while you are moving. It can then be returned to you once you have settled into your new home.

Now it is time to pull together all of your packing materials and secure all your belongings, prior to loading it up into the moving vehicle. You will need to carefully assess all of the smaller items that need packing and then sort out the cardboard boxes that you will be using as containers for these items. It is important to gather various size boxes since you will want all of your items to be tightly packed inside them to reduce movement during transportation and moving.

Boxes can be found at various place, such as supermarkets and department stores, but you may be better off getting clean boxes from a moving company that have been designed specifically for the purpose of moving. For example, you can get cardboard boxes with hanging bars so you can hang your clothes and reduce the chances of wrinkling them.

The added benefit of purchasing clean boxes from a moving company is that most moving companies will refund you some of your money if you return any unused boxes, or even used boxes that are still in good condition. Another piece of advice to remember is to always overestimated your needs than under-estimate them.

The last thing you want is to run out of packing material on the day of your move and have nothing to pack those last minute items you were using the night before moving out. Once you know how many boxes you are going to need, it will also help you to determine the size of the truck you will need.

When you choose the size of the van you are going to hire, you will need to determine whether you will need a tail-lift. This will cost you a few additional dollars, but it will also help save your back. This will prevent potential injuries since you won't have to lift heavy objects such as a heavy washing machine three feet in the air to load it into the back of the truck.

Again, if you have friends who have just moved recently, find out if they hired a van or truck and learn from their experience. Use the Internet to find truck rental companies and compare pricing. Even better look for companies that offer online reviews.

They may not all be 100% correct, but if you pay attention to the negative reviews, you may see a few red flags that you may want to consider before hiring a truck. If you are going to do the move yourself, you should try to enlist the help of family and friends, especially to help you move the large and heavy items.

Not all this will save you money, it can also potentially help you save your furniture from damage when they are being dropped or dragged because you didn't have enough hands on deck. Don't focus all of your energy on working out how you are going to move everything out from your old home to the new one.

There are other items that need to be taken care of. Such as notifying the utilities companies of your impending move. Be sure to let them know the date you will be vacating the premises and ask to read the meter on that day while you are still there, if possible.

Also make sure the utility companies supplying your new home are aware of the day you are taking up residence to ensure you are able to utilize these services immediately.

Be sure to give your landlord (if you are renting) adequate notice of your impending move. The amount of time would be determined by what is written in your lease.

Always be sure to leave your old home in a clean and presentable condition. You never know when you are going to need assistance from your old landlord (e.g. forwarding mail, giving references, etc.), so leave him or her with a good lasting impression of you.

Finally make sure the post office knows of your forwarding address in advance of your leaving date. They can then automatically forward any written correspondence to new address. Also contact any creditors you may have (your doctor, dentist, attorney and other important contacts) to let them know your new address.

This could save you any headaches from missing deadlines because of the delay in redirecting your email. If you follow these tips then you will surely have fewer headaches and stress. Then you will truly be able to enjoy your hot bath safe in the knowledge that you completed everything as planned.

Maintenance costs and taxes on the property is added up, and when there is an empty property, then a special vacant home insurance will have to be paid for by the owners of such a property. Attorney John Kopp also said that the heir or present owners can resume the preliminary work pertaining to a sale, which may include carrying out interviews with the real estate agents and repairs on the property.

This will require financial strength and a lot of time while they wait for the will to be probated and the official naming of the executor, which can be a very tedious process. It is recommended that the heirs of inherited properties should include a lawyer, who is familiar with both real estate law and, if possible, estates in general.

The process of searching for this type of lawyer and the expenses involved will obviously be a very stressful one. If there is no such estate lawyer to stand as a representative for the person who inherited the property, than expensive legal mistakes are bound to made.

Also, the named executor will have to be honest and trustworthy in dealing with the property. Before selling an inherited property, the property will have to pass through probate.

A probate is a way of showing proof that , what a legal document says about an individual's belongings when they die, is valid. Most countries allow summary probate, which is a quick process that doesn't take a long time or need any form of legal counsel.

But this option is only for small estates with low values. Unfortunately, other real estate assets exceed the low value, which means inherited properties like a house has to wait until the regular probate process is concluded before such property can be put on the market for sale and take a long time.

If an inherited property does not pass through probate, then the executor of the will cannot be given the authority to share the property, act or even settle outstanding debts.

If an executor has a siblings who will share in the property, the inherited property cannot be sold without the permission of both the court and the siblings. In many circumstances, elderly homeowners do not always maintain their homes.

In such cases, this makes things difficult for their heirs when things like heating, plumbing septic systems and carpets are outdated and need updating. For instance, a pending sale on a house might not go through, if after in inspecting the house, an oil tank is leaking underground and needs to be repaired. In this circumstances, you might have to sell the house at a lower price due to maintenance issues and concerns.

Sometimes, even decently repaired houses are crowded with a lifetime of belongings. In such cases, the heir to the house will have to make repairs, clean out the late person's belongings and make necessary updates on the home.

This may require an inspector who will recommend repairs for both present and potential threats before selling the house. Hiring an inspector can be time and resource consuming especially for heirs who live far from the inherited home. Once the necessary repairs and updates made on the inherited home, you calculate the total expenses and up may find that a small fortune has been spent.

This will have a great effect on trying to sell the house. You cannot afford to sell below the market value of the home and other maintenance costs. This can cause the heir to hike the price of the property above what it is truly worth.

The sale of a property like this can be difficult because it is really expensive and the price might be a barrier to potential buyers, thereby causing the property to take a longer time before it can be sold.

According to agents, clearing out houses usually involves many stages and processes. The number one thing to do is for the families to search and remove any relevant or essential heirlooms, papers, documents and expensive items that are found.

This process may take days. After this, an auction or a consignment shop can be contacted for sale of valuable items at fees at average around 25% to 30% of the sale amount. The other items that are not sold can then be given away or donated to charity organizations.

This could be a very tedious task because the heir to the house could be living far from the property's location, thus, making it difficult to locate a charity establishment around that vicinity.

Also, items that are not important or of less value that are left can be hauled out by a cleaning company at prices which are dependent on the contents of the house to be carried away, then the price may be really expensive.

Those heirs who live outside the country will have to heavily rely on the help of real estate agents for regular supervision of ongoing activities in their absence. One very difficult thing to do when you want to sell a home is to clear out the contents of the house, especially when the deceased has lived in it for a very long time, filling the house with lots of relevant and irrelevant things.

The reason for this difficulty is that it takes a period of time to figure out what each heir gets in cases where there is more than one heir to that house, which is one complicating factor.

For example, it could be really complicated when there are three or more siblings who inherit a home because each will have a different opinion on the price the property should be sold for. Also, multiple heirs will have differing opinions on the inspection of the house and the type of attorney need because each sibling will have different values and meanings in mind.

In tax consideration, after selling the inherited property, the tax basis for the home is the value of the home on the day the owner of the willed property died. The difference of the home's value and amount received after the sale of the property is the gain and on which taxes are owed.

CHAPTER 4
DOWNSIDES TO INHERITING

Although gifting a house to children is a very good thing, there are some negative implications that they have to figure out and try to fix if, they want to sell each inherited properties.

Sometimes a house is not inherited by just one child in the family, as there may be other children of the same parents. So trying to sell such a house may be difficult because it it not owned by one person.

You will have to notify other siblings about the decision to sell inherited property. This may lead to either a disagreement or an agreement among them because it is a joint property.

There are always potential issue=s whom there is more than one heir of an inherited property. One sibling may want the property sold and another wants it not be to sold. This type of disagreement can lead to disputes among the heirs of the property.

Also, when there is more than one owner of an inherited home, there can be a conflict over the pricing and strategy to be used for marketing it.Often times, the sellers not only have to deal with the sale of the house, but they are often mourning the deceased and at the same time trying to figure out how to best handle the estate.

They are going through hard times and have to try to make reasonable decisions at the same time, and this might take a whole lot of time to get over with. After inheriting a home from a deceased person, selling the home is not the same as other real estate transaction.

Clifton attorney, John Kopp who has recently sold his dead mother-in-law and mother's homes said, "it is not a bad idea to sell inherited properties in no time. Taking a quick decision on an estate property early is always better than later because of the carrying charges you have."

Maintenance costs and taxes on the property is added up, and when there is an empty property, then a special vacant home insurance will have to be paid for by the owner of such a property. Attorney John's Kepp also said that the heir or present owners can resume the preliminary work pertaining to a sale, which may include carrying out interviews with the real estate agents and repairs on the property.

This will require financial strength and a lot of time while they wait for the will to be probated and the official naming of the executor, which can be a very tedious topic. It is recommended that the heirs of inherited properties should include a lawyer, who is familiar with both real estate law and, if possible, estates in general.

The process of searching for this type of lawyer and the expenses involved will obviously be a very stressful one. If there is no such estate lawyer to stand as a representative for the who inherited the property, then expensive legal mistakes are bound to be made.

Also, the named executor will have to be honest and trustworthy in dealing with the property. Before selling an inherited property, the property will have to pass through probate.

A probate is a way of showing proof that, what a legal document says about an individual's belongings when they die, is valid.Most countries allow summary probate, which is a quick process that doesn't take a long time or need any form of legal counsel.

But this options is only for small estates with low values. Unfortunately, other real estate assets exceed the low value, which means inherited properties like a house has to wait until the regular probate process is concluded before such property can be put on the market for sale and take a long time.

If an inherited property does not pass through probate, then the executor of the will cannot he gives the authority to share the property, act or even settle outstanding debts.

If an executor has siblings who will share in the property, the inherited property cannot be sold without the permission of both the court and the siblings. In many circumstances, elderly homeowners do not always maintain their homes.

In such cases, this makes things difficult for the heirs when things like heating, plumbing, septic systems and carpets are outdated and need updating. For instance, a pending sale on a house might not go through if after inspecting the house, an oil tank is leaking underground and needs to be repaired. In this, circumstances, you might have to sell the house at a lower price due to maintenance issues and concerns.

Sometimes, even decently repaired homes are crowded with a lifetime of belongings. In such cases, the heir to the house will have to make repairs, clean out the late person's belongings and make necessary updates on the home.

This may require an inspector who will recommend repairs for both present and potential threats before selling the house. Hiring as inspector can be time and resource consuming especially for heirs who live far from the inherited home. Once the necessary repairs and updates are made on the inherited house, you calculate the total expenses and up may find out that a small fortune has been spent.

This will have a great effect on trying to sell the house. You cannot afford to sell below the market value of the home and other maintenance costs. This can cause the heir to hike the price of the property above that it is truly worth.

The sale of a property like this can be very difficult because it is really expensive and the price might be a barrier to potential buyers, thereby causing the property to take a longer before it can be sold.

According to agents, clearing and cleaning out houses usually involves many stages and processes. The number one thing to do is for the families to search and remove any relevant or essential heirlooms, papers, documents and expensive item that are found.

This process may take days. After this, an auction or a consignment shop can contracted for sale of valuable items at fees that average around 25% to 30% of the sale amount. The other items that are not sold can be given away or donated to charity organizations.

This could be a very tedious task because the heir to the house could be living far from the property's location, thus, making it difficult to locate a charity establishment around that vicinity.

Also, items that are not important or of less value that are left can be hauled out by a clearing company at prices which are dependent on the contents of the house and sizes of items to be hauled away. So if there are many items to be carried away, then the price may be really expensive.

Those heirs who live outside the country will have to heavily rely on the help of real estate agents for regular supervision of ongoing activities in their absence. One very difficult thing to do when you want to sell a home is to clear out the contents of the house, especially when the deceased has lived in it for a very long time, filling the house with lots of relevant and irrelevant things.

The reason for this difficulty is that it takes a period of time to figure out what each heir gets in cases where there is more than one heir to the house, which is one complicating factor.

For example, it could be really complicated when there are three or more siblings who inherit a home because each will have a different opinion on the price the property should be sold for. Also, multiple heirs will have differing opinions on the inspection of the house and the type of attorney need because each sibling will have different values and meanings in mind.

In tax consideration, after selling the inherited property, the tax basis for the home is the value of the home on the day the owner of the willed property died. The difference of the home's value and amount received after the sale of the property is the gain and on which taxes are owed.

When more than one sibling inherits the home, the gain is divided equally and each heir will claim the share on taxes. So if sales value of the property is lesser than the value of the property before sales, then there will be no gain to be reported.

Although it may be necessary to use much money on very important renovations such as new toilets, bathrooms and kitchen modelling, selling such a house will be almost impossible especially inherited building is not in a favorable environment and the amenities are outdated.

CHAPTER 5
HOW SELLING A HOUSE IN AN ESTATE DIFFERS FROM REGULAR SALES

A probate sale begins once someone has passed away, even if there is no will in effect at their time of death. If you have a living trust, however, you can bypass the lengthy and costly process of probate fees, which include attorney, court, and arbitrator fees.

In total, these fees can take at least 6% of the overall estate value, whether it's boats, cars, bank savings, retirement funds, securities, personal items, and the real estate itself. However, you can proceed with the actual probate by yourself if that is what you want to do.

The court clerk for your area will give you all of the forms to fill out that you are going to need, with one of them being needed to publish to any and all creditors that will be involved. If real estate is involved in the will of the person who is deceased, the executor may request themselves to be nominated through whichever estate act in place in your state, so the property in the will not have to go through the confirmation process in court.

This will help to save both money and time, as they will list it and sell it like they would any other home. The executor will accept the best offer, then proceed to sign and close the deal when going through the process like any other real estate transaction, but without all requirements for real estate transfer disclosure.

Although, just as a precaution, the executor or the administrator will need to have any other heir sign a waiver for the notice of the proposed action.

Because of the fact that the courts are involved with probate selling, trust and probate sales have an entirely different vocabulary of their own when compared to regular real estate.

Probate sales also involve multiple contracts and disclosure statements that are never used with types of real estate transactions. If you are buying or selling real property through a probate transaction, then you absolutely must use a real estate agent who has experiences with these types of transactions, which include trust sales.

They includes all of the steps and the documentation that come with these types of transactions as clear communication with probate sales is critically vital.

Typical Steps Explained Further for Probate Buying and Selling Transactions

In the majority of cases, when it comes to probate buying and selling, the decedent's will have named an executor to handle all of the distribution of assets, including any real estate property. However, if the deceased has not named an executor in the will, the executor that is named does not want to handle the real estate, or if there is no will, period, the court will appoint an administrator to handle all of the duties.

The administrator or the executor is in charge when it comes to listing and selling the property, as the sale will not be able to proceed until one has been identified and confirmed. As stated in the Independent Administration of Estates Act, or the IAEA, the executor will established a listed price for the real estate property, which take into account the appraisal that will be taken from probate arbitrator.

This is typically determined through assistance with a real estate agent, who must be experienced when it comes to trust and probate sales. From there, the property is listed for sale with a real estate agent or real estate broker.

The real estate agent the aggressively markets the real estate property to the public to attract the best, obviously the highest, offer, which will involve multiple approaches.

These include newspaper advertising, signage, hosting open houses for any potential buyers and other real estate agents, and listing the property on more than one website for real estate properties.

The real estate agent is also in charge of scheduling all appointments when it comes to showing the property to any interested parties directly inquiring. Even though buyers of trust and probate real estate are probably looking for a bargain, the offers in range can be pretty limited by the court.

An offer that is accepted must be 90%, or even more, of the appraised value by the probate referee. The real estate agent then help the seller once a buyer has been found in the negotiation of the terms, which must be satisfactory for both the buyer and the seller.

Once the property offer has been accepted, a noticed proposed action is then mailed out to all of the heirs involved, which states all of the terms for the proposed sale. The heirs will then have 15 days to look over the notice themselves and make any objections known.

If no objections are stated, the sale can proceed without needing a court hearing. If the administrator or executor does not have full independent power under the IAEA, or if an heir has and states an objection over the notice of proposed action, the notice for the sale is then published into a generally distributed newspaper for that area, unless the will states that action cannot be mandated.

The real estate's attorney the makes an application for the confirmation hearing court date once the sale is to be executed, which is usually within 30 to 40 days of the certain date when the application was filed. A copy of the details and the application itself concerning the property are then mailed to all of the interested and participating parties.

The real estate broker, even after there has been a confirmed court date set, will continue to hold showing of the property, and advertise the property to all potential buyers to secure an over-bidder, for the purpose of raising the price of sale.

Once the court confirmation hearing takes place, any previously accepted bid can be overbid by another interested party.

If such a case happens, the party overbidding must be present at the hearing and bring a cashier's check, it cannot be a personal one, with the amount that is totaled over 10% of the minimum price for overbidding, in order to overbid successfully.

The minimum bed is always determined by using a formula of 10% of the beginning $10,000 with an additional 5% of the overall balance for the accepted offer.

If you go with an over-bidder instead of the original buyer, you will have to return the initial deposit that they have made, which should be done as soon as you accept the over-bidder's offer to avoid any problems and disputes with you as the seller.

However, there be more than one person present to overbid, the highest bidder will win the real estate property, and will give their cashier's check over to the administrator or the executor.

From there, an escrow account and will close between 30 to 40 days after the court hearing has ended.

Getting Yourself Ready to Hand Over the Keys

Selling a piece of property that was inherited by you from a loved one is never easy, so make sure you take the necessary time you need to clear out all of the belongings and further depersonalized each room.

This process will be a lot harder to do than the actual selling, so it is perfectly fine to take your time. You should also bring in a contractor, plumber, and an electrician to ensure that everything in the house is in perfect order.

If there are problems, make sure that you take care of the updates or repairs before you approve and start any showings to potential buyers. This will help give you a better chance of selling as soon as possible.

If you drag your feet with the depersonalizing process, that is fine, but you can only do so for a limited time. It's better to get this out of the way as soon as possible so you can move on.

CHAPTER 6
DETERMINING THE PROPER VALUE OF AN INHERITED HOME

Before you can even think about determining the value of your inherited home, you first must know what not to do during the entire process of selling it.

Not Hiring an Agent Because You Feel You Don't Need One

Don't do this, you need an agent. Even though there is a 6% commission involved, trying to sell this home on your own, especially if you do not have any real estate experience, will be a complete nightmare.

A decent real estate agent will help you stick to your selling price once the home has been valued, which will greatly increase your odds for a pain-free sale.

A decent real estate agent will also take some of the stress and high emotions out of the process for you, through interacting directly with all potential buyers while you can focus on other things.

Your real estate agent will eliminate any "buyers" who only have the intention of browsing your property just to look and not buy. It can be incredibly stressful with people like this, but with an agent, you won't even have to think about it.

They will only hiring people who are 100% serious to your attention. A real estate agent will have a lot more experience than you do when it comes to the negotiation process, which will potentially help you to get the most amount of money possible.

Plus, if any issues come up during this process, and they usually do, your agent will handle them for you. This includes both difficulties and paperwork during the real estate transaction.

Some people do sell their own homes without pulling out their hair, but that's only because they have some experience and probably have help from someone other than an agent.

However, when it comes to inherited properties, it's better to have an agent and some help on your side, as this process is not the same as selling your own home.

Do Not Get Emotionally Involved

Clearly, you are selling this home for a reason, so getting emotionally involved is the absolute worst thing you could do. Begin to think of yourself as a businessperson and not the homeowner.

From this point, until the transaction is signed and completely done, you are a home seller and need to act and do accordingly.

If you begin looking at this transaction completely from a financial perspective, you will distance yourself farther away from any emotional aspect of selling this property you've probably had many memories in.

One way to avoid this is to make the home look completely different. Repaint every room, take away all pictures and any memorabilia, and anything else that make the house feel like a home. This will work to your advantage and make the home feel empty to you, but new and exciting for potential buyers.

Don't Sell During Winter

Around the holidays especially, home sales take a huge drop. So wait until the spring or even the summer to list the inherited home. Because of the cold weather and social engagements, people will be busy and won't have time to drive around and look at homes.

Therefore, selling during warmer seasons is the best way to ensure you get what you're asking for with the sale price, and to ensure you sell the inherited property faster.

Determining the value of the Inherited Home

There are multiple ways to determine the value of the inherited home when it comes to fairness for home market value for tax purposes.

Speak with a Reputable Appraiser

To get the most accurate and fair market value report price, go speak with a professional, certified, and reputable appraiser. They will look over the property and determine if there are any complications that need to be resolved, such as issues with plumbing, or any comparable sale prices for homes in the overall general vicinity.

From there, they will give you an estimate as to what the inherited dome can be valued to.

Get a Couple of Real Estate Agents

This is typically a free option, where you need to actually hire an appraiser for a walk through. If you have a couple of real estate agents do a separate walk through, obviously never at the same time, they will give you an estimate that is more true to fair market value.

Typically, a real estate agent will agree to do an appraiser because they believe that this will be a good way to get your listing, and your commission.

Do Your Own Research

You could also do a little groundwork yourself by looking through multiple internet listing services.

This will help you see what you're up against in regards to price comparisons, so you can be sure that one agent is not just wooing you with an expectation that is not realistic.

This will also help you to see what other are listing their properties for in the area, what their homes have that you inherited home does not, and what your general value should be.

Get in Touch with the Executor

This may not apply to everyone, as sometimes a specific executor has not been named in the will. However, if an executor was, then you can do this. Contact the specified executor of the deceased's will and ask him or her whether or not he is elected to have an alternate date for determining the cost basis.

Executor might decide to use a specific date of six months after the death of the decedent to value the home. However, if he or she has not decided to go forth with an alternate, only then will the date of death be used for valuing the inherited home.

Using the Cost Basis

If the decent passed away in 2015, the cost basis will carry over, which will be used for the original cost basis of the home and used as the value. This could be for the purchase price, or for a step-up cost basis if the property was given to them as an inheritance.

There is a step-up total basis of $1.3 million or another of $4.3 million for any surviving spouse, which will increase the cost basis and value.

This basis increase will be applied to the overall inheritance itself, and not just the real estate involved. Therefore, you can use all or none for the real estate, and get the value elsewhere.

Steps to Selling Your Inherited Home

Selling an inherited home from a loved one can be an emotional process, so avoiding obstacles that waste of money, add to your frustration and lose time are incredibly important.

Preparing the Home

Once the selling decision has made and all financial implications have been dealt with your real estate agent, you can begin preparing the home.

You will need to completely depersonalize the home for sale quality, and for peace of mind. Start by cleaning out all of the personal belongings, but ensure that you take your time, considering this will be emotionally challenging and one of the disadvantages of inheriting a home.

You will probably discover things that bring up memories of the past, things you want to keep, and other meaningful items, which is going to be difficult. It's important to take time you need for this process.

If there are things you want to sell, after you have divided all of the possessions that you want to take as the heir, hold a yard sale or an estate sale for the rest.

Homes tend to show better on the market when they are staged or completely empty, but make sure it's completely clean. Bring in a cleaning service if you have to.

Once the home is ready, your next step should be to find the perfect real estate agent for your situation. They should be knowledgeable and experienced with selling inherited homes. Make sure that you're looking into the right ones before you make any phone calls or meet with them. Do not ask friends and family for a recommendation, unless they have used this real estate agent to help them with selling an inherited home.

Speak with the real estate agent about waiting for the estate to go through the probate process. In short, your inherited home must go through the probate process before you can sell it, but it's best to ask them about what you should expect during this period.

The majority of states have a process of summary probate, but only for small properties that range in a few thousand dollars in value. Typically, most estates with real estate will exceed this threshold, especially if they have other assets involved with them.

Next, determine who specifically has the legal responsibility in regards to handling this transaction. If the deceased has a will and stated an executor as the one with the responsibility for disturbing all of the assets of their estate, including the real estate, then you need to be in touch. If the property is within a trust, however, the trustee has the power.

In the case of siblings having responsibility for this transaction, if the home has been left to them by the last remaining parent, for example, one will usually take authority and responsibility over the other to handle the real estate transaction.

Once all of this is done, get your asking price by comparing similar properties. Depending on the conditions of the market for either buying or selling, you may see offers that are thousands of dollars below your asking price.

Now that you have real estate agent working with you, negotiations will be incredibly easy, because they will help you through this process and give you guidance on what you should do. You should not expect to receive your asking price, but set the price around what you would generally be happy selling it at especially if offers are below your asking price.

Overall, the process of negotiation will determine the final selling price. Therefore, your real estate agent selection should be someone who will not only advocate for you, but negotiate on your behalf, as well, considering this is incredibly important, and should not be done lightly.

At the same time do not price the inherited property too high, as it will drive potential buyers away. Make the price as realistic as possible, but at a price that is higher than what you are willing to settle on. Even still, do not settle for a price that you're uncomfortable with, and don't jump on the first offer you get excited over. Always go over each individual offer with your real estate agent before you make your decision.

Don't Be Surprised If...

- Executors keep the estate in probate for years, for use of assets.

- In this case, speak with your real estate agent about what you can do should this situation occur.

- The will states that the home and all other assets and property is to be divided equally between beneficiaries, which means the overall value must be equally distributed.

- You eventually feel guilty about the possessions you chose not to keep. Don't worry, this is natural, and you should expect it to happen regardless, but don't feel obligated to try and get them back, no matter how badly you feel.

CHAPTER 7
DISTRIBUTION AMONG FAMILY MEMBERS

T he most decent and courteous manner of equally dividing the inheritance from a deceased family member would follow accordingly:

#1. Select Items that You or Your Family Members Intend to Keep

The first step requires time and energy to go through every item in the house that you or your family members intend to keep. It is a grave loss, and painful feeling to endure the loss of a loved one, not to mention going through all their possessions they have left.Before moving on to next step in selling or auctioning the items, it is crucial to establish a boundary or limit to whoever possesses the right to keep the sentimental items or properties between the family members capacity among siblings.If the deceased family member left a will, then all should be abided by what is started within that will, otherwise by controlling state law or law of intestate succession if there is no will written.If the will or law requires the property to be divided equally, then you must follow it.For better organization, you are encouraged to separate the items you wish to keep in a separate container or at your place to avoid confusion of selling, donating or throwing away the objects.Mutual agreement between your siblings or other family members cum come into terms of who will keep the sentimental objects without having any disputes. There is an algorithm developed to fairly distribute an inheritance among the siblings within a family. The algorithm developed is to divide the inheritance between them equally. There are a number of items ranging from furniture, clothes, jewelry, to the house itself.

The family can resort to working with a modulator to resolve a fair distribution of items or properties between the family members or siblings.

This would be a fair system when the family does not wish to liquidate the assets or rejects joint ownership between the siblings. However, only under following circumstances will the algorithm be carried one effectively and fairly.

Each family member will receive the same number of items. There are some items that may not be assigned to any of the members, and will require time for further consultation consideration outside of this algorithm. Each member then will submit his or her own prioritized list of items to the mediator.

After the allocation, the mediator will prepare a list for each member of the family of the items allocated for each of them.

Each member will then show their list of preferred items to the other members.

It is important to make that it is not completely compulsory for you to store or keep any of the items your loved ones left behind unless the items really possesses sentimental value or is significant to you. In this way, you will not become a border by keeping any items inside your home that takes up living space unnecessarily.

If you come across any papers, be sure to thoroughly review each one before proceeding to throw them out.

Important key financial documents such as wills, trust, addenda, real estate deeds and title should be kept. A simple tip on what items you should keep is to preserve any sentimental photos or memorabilia that are irreplaceable.

#2* Sell Any Valuable Items or Properly andDistribute the Net Profit Equally

In a scenario where you and your siblings have inherited real estate from your deceased parents, it is important in seek mutual terms as to whether the property should be sold and split the profit immediately or simply keep and share the use of the house.

Any auction or estate sale company would recommend that you keep every single item in the house before discarding them. People will pay you for these items, plus it saves you time and hassle of throwing them out. In certain circumstance have no interest in it.

Non-pro rata distribution or equal division of value is the option if there are other assets in the estate. Through this agreement, the one who wants the house gets to keep it while the others get cash or other assets, but ultimately everyone will receive equal value of assets.

The final option would be that the sibling who wants the house would simply have to buy out the other siblings interest in it. You may also seek professional advice such as from real estate investors, agents or attorneys.

They can give your personal views or feedback on how to sell your house at the highest possible value the market. Information you might want to look out for is the cost basis, what is owned on the house or any outstanding lines.

They can help you in making selling decisions. You can hire an estate appraiser to value furniture, jewelry and antiques.

Such professional can provide you an estimate for any valuable item, charging an hourly fee depending on location of the house, and type of appraisal you want.

To find a trustworthy appraiser, you can do online research and see their credentials.

Nowadays, It is a more convenient, and common practice to sell any unwanted items that you wish to throw out while earning extra cash online.

Another traditional method would be simply to sell it in public such as having an estate sale. Here is a tip on running an effective sale in your neighborhood: price every single item you want to sell.

Seek extra hands to help you conduct the business such as running the cash box, or help in promoting and selling the items. Remember that when you are running the sale, you will be doing it for more than a day, at most four days.

Make sure to do online advertising in your community to get word out about your sale.

This will help to attract more customers from areas close by to come to your sale. It is important that you do not post the location of thesale until the very day itself to avoid any suspicious people snooping around the house looking at the items or the possibility of theft and robbery.

You can share the location of the city or district to let people know the venue, and then you share the address on the day you wish to make a sale. Certain cities require some sort of permit for holding a sale. Do ensure that you comply with the local authorities.

It would be helpful for the customers if you post signs or directions in the neighborhood to assist people in directing them towards your sale.

If you are unable to sell all of your remaining items on the last day of your sale, it is recommended that you set 50% discount price, or simply give it away for free.

However, if running an estate sale is too much of burden for you or your family members to handle, you can hire an estate sale or auction company to handle the sale for you.

They will get paid based on the percentage of the sales after they have quoted it with you upfront. Expect to pay at least 30% to 50% of the entire profit of the sale.

Another option would be so hire an estate liquidation company to handle a sale. A liquidator is someone you can hire to clear off any items you don't intend to keep, and have decided to sell, discard or donate.

Nevertheless, it is critical that you would interview the firms to find the most reliable, credible and qualified company since the industry is rarely regulated, thus having little training or experience.

Like searching for real estate agent, it is important that you do a background check on the company, search for contract information, and call any previous clients regarding their opinions and experiences of working with them.

Typical estate liquidators keep about 35% to 40% of the sales profit, but this percentage can vary depending on service offered.

So, discuss with the company regarding the research, appraisal and price of your items, duration of the sale, and how much agonizing with the buyers it will do.

You may also do a clean-up or catalog each items so that you might sell in a garage sale or estate sale.

Discuss the clean-up plan after the sale has ended such as clearing out items or cleaning services to determine if required any additional fees.

If you are not been to sell the house, you may also rent it out. You and your siblings can benefit from the profit shares while still possessing ownership of the house.

This will also give additional time to gather thoughts and discuss among each other to decide on the new phase in ownership of the property.

#3. Donate Any Recyclable Items to Those in Need

At certain point, you may find yourself wanting to donate certain items either during or after the sale.

Donation can be beneficial, as it is a general charitable act to help those in need instead of simply during items away into a dumpster. You have options of donation junk to emphanagoes, the homeless, or disaster victims.

Items that you no longer need can either be cloths, book, cutlery or even toys. Sometimes, you can request a transport service truck if you wish to donate a lot of unwanted items.

It is a great way to give back to the community, and to be rewarded for a kind act. Furthermore, you can also good tax deductions for your contribution. The available tax deduction to the donor depends in part on the donor's items value, which is the value of the items for taxation purpose at the time that it is inherited.

Bear in mind that if a charitable donation is not exactly authorized in a will or trust, the estate may not proper take a deduction for the donation.

So, the estate is not eligible for deduction for the transfers to charity by the beneficiaries, even if their integrations were good.

However, the individuals may donate certain item, which were passed to them from an estate and can claims a charitable deduction on their personal tax returns.

An income tax deduction for a charitable contribution donation of assets is normally the fair market value of that asset, minus any appreciation or capital gain.

The value of the charitable deduction depends on the time the property was acquired. you must also consider the laws in your local area regarding charitable donation and estate taxes, since these may change at times, There may be additional regulation regarding taxation on estate and property transfers.

Community property states have different rules for the calculation of value of the property inherited from family members. It is advisable to consult with a local certified tax professional to assure that you donation of inherited property is carried out in the most economical and efficient manner in accordance to time and place of your donation.

If you are unsure or confused about tax deduction for charitable and estates, you should refer to your attorney or online for better understanding.

#4. Throw Away Any Remaining Items that Have NoSignificant or Sentimental Value

After you had gone through the processes of separating items for yourself, for your family members, for sale and for donation, the last step to finally clear the remaining items, would be to throw them away.

Remaining junk can vary in size and the proper way to discard them depends on the moment of junk as well. You may fit them in garbage bags or empty boxes and safely discard at the nearest despicable waste area. You might need to call your local garbage pickup service to dispose of the items properly if you line up piles of garbage at the street curb. Otherwise, the garbage men may simply ignore it. Depending on the city you reside in, there may be a fee for this service, but it doesn't hurt to do a bit of research, Charges may include delivery and pickup of a dumpster when it is full.

A helpful tip would be in get the largest damper than you need because there is a high chance that it may fill up quickly. Clearing old items out will require extra time and energy. you may need extra hands to do some clean up. An alternative would be to hire a junk removal company that can provide both dumpster or dump truck and labor.

Last reminder before throwing away old items is in always ensure that you would never regret discarding them unless they possess any sentimental value at all. Otherwise, It is wise to donate it if no one wishes to buy it from you.

In life, nothing can tear a family apart more than money. Honesty and integrity will play an important role in the distribution of the inheritance between families as well.

Despite careful planning and a will to guide the inheritance distribution, this is a subjective and sensitive matter in terms of rights and ownership.

Another way is to assign specific interns that will go to a specific person in a letter of instruction. you could also act up a process for the heirs to use to decide who gets what, for example letting the executor decide, sell the disputed object by force and distribute the money equally. last resort should be to put all items up for auction and let heirs bid on them first.

Favoritism can also lead in dispute between siblings unless the parents can show fairness and impartiality towards their children. Open floor discussions between parents and growing children will be great alternatives to explain the inheritance distributions.

Issues or any objections can be discussed instantly with reason and understanding imply fairness.

At certain times, you may need to provide extra support in life to one of your heirs while others may be financially stable.

Your inheritance needs to be allocated to your heirs such as shares from a family business in proportion to their workload.

CHAPTER 8
4 WAYS TO SELL YOUR HOUSE

W hether you are moving to another part of the city, or you inherited a house, there are many ways to sell it. Some are good, and some aren't which means that your have to be very careful when you are selling your house.

Pick the wrong way or do something wrong and you will be left with no house and little money, basically you will be left with nothing (or not much) to show for it. In many ways the methods that are selected in this short list are the best, although every technique has its own pros and cons.

Auction

Selling a house at an auction can prove to be very profitable, An auction is an advanced method and it is great tool for quick sell with the least amount of hustle.

There are a few different types of auction. Normally there are multiple buyers bidding for the house at the same time and whoever offers the most money wins the house. Typically, the auction is announced with 2-3 weeks notices.

In those few weeks it is standard practice that 1-2 days are reserved for open house preview. In those couple of days, people can come to the house, check it out and see if it meets their needs, it is pretty logical, because there would be no sense in bidding un a house that you have just seen for the first time several minutes prior to the start of the auction

Before even thinking about yelling "SOLD" you have to contact an auctioneer.

It is very important to choose the right one. they will advise you about the value of the property, the guide price and the reserve price. The guide price is an indication of what the house's reserve price is, although it isn't necessarily the figure the property will be sold.

The reserve price is the bare minimum you are willing to accept for your property.

This is a method that will prevent you from losing money or be left with less than your were hoping for. If the reserve price isn't achieved, you won't have to sell the house. You are only obligated to sell if the reserve price is met.

Everything should be prepared at least a week before the auction. You can sell the house with all the things inside, like furniture, but be sure to take everything you don't want to sell.

You don't want to lose your precious memories, and it is highly unlikely that new buyers will ever use your already used towels. Selling what was once your home can be tough, so make sure your really want to do it.

The most important thing is to be absolutely sure that you want to sell the house. Once the auction starts it will be almost impossible in win the house back, unless you bid higher than anytime.

The auction usually takes place at the house that is being sold. Before the can actually start, all the potential buyers (the bidders) are required to register and prove that they can pay for the property. you wouldn't want to sell your house to a burn.

That's why all the bidders show that verified funds are available as a deposit if they win. Once the auctioneer starts the bidding all you can do is watch. Whoever bids the highest is the winner.

They sign the purchase agreement and submit the deposit. Your house is sold before you can yell "SOLD" Well unless you are an auctioneer we know how fast they speak.

Pros

If buyers let connection take over, the bidding wars can be funded by them and drive the price very high. Competition and go often burst emotion. Nobody wants to lose to everyone just keep bidding.

People get caught up in the auction and end up paying far more than the actual value of the property.

The home is sold "as-is" ao no fixes and repairs are to be done by the seller, You can also leave anything that you don't spend, anything that you can't be bothered with, and i will be sold with the house. Other theme repairs, you also won't have to worry about city inspections, that's also the buyer's problem.

There are hardly any cuntigercies and the deposit is often fairly high. The buyer will and have a ways cost of the contract and he will have to deposit at least 10% contract price or $2,500 immediately after the auction.

If the property isn't closed on in 30 days or less, the buyer forfeits the deposit, which will ensure that only service buyers apply for the auction.

Cons

The biggest down ride of an auction is that it is unpredictable. The contome is uncertain and you can be left with much less than you were hoping for.

Forwardly, this can be previewed by writing a review rise also you will have to hire a skilled professional, and skills come with a price.

Sell to an Investor

There are many top-rated real estate investors in almost every city. They are always on the look for a new pardesi, therefore, you should be able to find one rather easily.

There is always something to beware of, and in this it's scams. There are many scams, which means that you need to find the Light investor in order not to get ripped off. When the right Investor is hired, typically one of his agents (or himself) will come and check out your house.

They are going to ask you a few questions about the house and give you a quick appraisal. Sometimes this process can be done over the phone, without having to meet. Real estate investors buy properties in order to make some cash, and you should always keep that in mind when you are selling to an investor.

They often buy house that need to be sold as quickly as possible. The houses are then repaired, everything is restored and is sold for far more money that it was brought for. That's why most of them are trying very hard to get lowest price possible when purchasing the house.

As it was mentioned earlier, some will every try to scam you, but that is why it is very important to hire an investor that is reliable and professional. Selling a house to an investor shouldn't really be your first choice.

It is only a primary choice if you're in hurry to sell the house. Sometimes you can get an offer on the house within only a couple of days and you can close the deal within a week.

It will almost always be quick and painless. Additionally. you won't get any unexpected, hidden fees and commissions, Investors make cash from selling the property, so you won't have to think about losing money on this kind of deal.

Pros

One of the biggest perks of selling a property to a real estate investor is that they will buy it *us is*, If the house is bought in *as-is* condition, you won't have to do any repairs by yourself.

Additionally, the investor is much more likely to buy a house that needs lots of repairs than the average buyer. An average buyer wants to move to the house and use it as soon as possible. The investor wants to give it a makeover and sell it for a profit.

Sometimes the investor won't even have to see the house because he intends on flipping it, so the deal can be made very efficiently.

A more dependable and quicker closing is also what comes from selling to an investor. In many cases, the deal can fall apart if the buyer suddenly runs out of money.

There are many reasons why this can happen, one of which is the very nature of the investment business. It can be very risky from time to time, and when the buyer backs out of the agreement, the seller can be left with nothing except for the house that he already wants to get rid of.

Many months can be wasted, and while the buyer wasted your time, you will have to spend money on stuff like insurance, taxes, mortgage, etc. Cash closing will prevent this from happening.

Even if the buyer runs out of money and he backs out of the deal, you will be left with the deposit, which means that your time won't be wasted after all. Other than being quick and dependable, selling to an investor can spare you of further fees and commissions.

If the deal is made without an agent, you can save on the commission, which is often 6% of the selling price. That can add up to quite a big number, depending on the property you sell.

There are many others fees that show up inthe fine print which you probably won't even know you are paying for, but this can't happen if you sell to an investor. By selling the house "as-is", you will be able to leave all the unwanted stuff in the house.

Everything you don't want in your new home can be left in the old one, and the investor will boy the whole package.

Cons

There aren't cons when it comes to selling to an investor, but the one that exists can sometimes make you regret contacting an investor.

The fact is that they try to make a profit from reselling property. In order for them to succeed in this, they will always try to buy the house for the lowest price possible.

I'm not saying that all of them are dishonest, but many willoffer you loss than the actual value of the house.

Many will use devious means in achieving their goal. The is almost no chance you'll get full value for your home in this situation, It's not suggested to sell to an investor unless you are in a dire situation.

For Sale by Owner

This method is by far the most unreliable and riskiest on this short list. For sale by owner means that you are selling property by yourself, without any help from professionals.

This means that you won't be hiring any licensed agent which, in most case, proves to be a mistake. People want to save some money on commission and fees, so they take this step into the unknown.

How hard can it be? Let me tell you that it can be very hard.

There is a reason professional exist and, if they were useless, people would stop hiring them. If everybody could do their job, there wouldn't exist the need for a professional real estate agent.

However, if you decide to sell yourself, there are certain preparations that need to be made. First of all, try to focus on web marketing. The best way to attract as many potential buyer as possible is through Internet and Social Media.

You will have to appeal to great number of people so that a lot of offers are made.

You should also repair everything in your home and put everything in order, so that the photos attract many potential customers. Making sure the price is right will ensure that you don't lose money.

This means that you will have to do a lot of research and hire an appraiser. To make sure you don't get hustled, you will probably have to hire a lawyer, too. Hiring all there people will make you wonder if this is really a way to save money.

Pros

You may be able to save some money on commissions and fee,but that won't guarantee you the profit that you expected.

Cons

First of all, without an agent the house might not get enough market exposure and advertising. This is essential if you want to attract buyers. Without the help of professional you might not be able to evaluate the property correctly.

If the price is too high, no one will want to buy it. Too low and you will be left with less cash than you expected.

This method is very time-consuming. It will take a lot of time to research the market, to advertise your house, and to make an appraisal.

You do everything by yourself and you have to pay attention to every detail.

In the for-sale-by-owner scenario nobody has your back. There are many things that can go wrong and if you are alone in it, you will have a really tough time.

You won't know if you're being scammed, you won't be able to cope with a buyer if he is a skilled agent and you probably aren't familiar with the real estate laws. there are so many more cons than pros when it comes to selling a house by yourself, therefore I wouldn't recommend it.

Hiring an Agent

The most common way of selling a property is to hire an agent . This might also be the safest and most reliable way. The way it works is that you first have to sign a listing agreement with an agent.

The contract the agent to a commission, which is usually 6% of the sales price. When this is done, the real estate agent will advertise the property. This way, many potential buyers will notice the house and possibly make an offer.

When an offer is made, you don't automatically sell and get the money. There is a process between getting an offer and receiving the check, and the agent is there to guide you through the process.

They will navigate the negotiations, appraisals and possible repairs. They do almost everything and you just have to sit back and relax.

Many listing agreements will be an "exclusive right to sell the contract" which means that regardless of who finds a buyer, the argent will get the full commission.

Once the contract is made with the buyer and the property is sold, the agent gets paid and you can forget about the house.

If you think that you could do this all by yourself and save some money, think again. Many people are trying to save as much as they can, and realistically, who wouldn't want to keep that 6% for themselves.

Do the math and it can be a lot of money. It can make you think that it is worthwhile to spend time and energy on something like this.

Nevertheless, the readily of the process is much different. Other than wasting year time and energy, you might also be spending more money than predicted.

By doing everything alone, you pay for every service, every professional, you pay for everything. Agent know the charged way to snake things happen and they know the most effective way to sell your house.

Their payment depends on their work, so you can be are you'll get the best service.

Pros

By hiring an agent, you will have an experienced professional to advise you and guide you through the whole process of selling the house. He will manage all the paperwork and do all the stuff you never knew had to be done.

Agents have tools and resources that simply aren't available to the general public. It's part of their job.

those tools help them sell your house effectively, by analyzing the marked trends and pricing the house accordingly and by projecting how long it will take to sell the property.

Agents will list the house on the marketplace known as multiple listing services (MLS).

This is the best marketplace for leasing and sealing properties, and only agents have access to it. Only real estate agents can list a house for sale on the MLS, and it is the most powerful and influential way to make the property available to the messes.

One of the best things about hiring an agent is that he can really highlight the best qualities of the property that is being sold. If there is something that needs to be repaired or ahead, the agent will be able to see it. This will help you sell the house faster and it will help increase its value.

Cons

The commission fee is the only negative, but most of the time you'll save more in the long run working with an agent.

CHAPTER 9
INHERITED HOME TAX

Whenever you sell a home, you should understand that special tax rules apply if the house you are selling is inherited.

So many people ask themselves if they will be excepted from the hundreds of thousands of dollars of taxes if they sell a house they inherited. The simple answer is no.

Selling a house that you inherited does not exempt you from any of the taxes. The only benefit that you get in the stepped-up basis rules for any property that is inherited.

Therefore, that means that whenever you sell an inherited property or a home, you are not excluded from the taxes. the tax law provides homeowners with very generous tax exclusions when they sell their property.Up to $250,000 of any gain from such a sale received by a single homeowner is tax-free. For married homeownersfiling jointly. up to $500,000 of gain is excluded from income.

To qualify for the exclusion, the home must have been used as the main home for two years out of the prior five years before the sale. At the time you inherit a home, you will not quality for this exclusion. you will have to move into the home and live there for at least two years to be eligible.

However, you many not really need the exclusion because of the stepped-up basis rules.

Basis means an asset's cost for tax purpose. To determine whether you have a profit or loss when you sell a property, you subtract its basis from the sale price.

If you have a positive number, you have a gain. If you have a negative number, you have a loss. the basis of a home you buy or build is its cost, plus any improvements you make while you own it. See Determining your Home's Tax Basis for details.

However, a home's tax basis is defined in a different way when someone inherits a home after the owner dies.

When you inherit property after the owner dies, you automatically receive a stepped-up basis. This means that the home's cost for tax purpose is not what the now-deceased owner paid for it, Instead, its basis is its fair market value at the time of the prior owner's death.

This will usually be more that the prior owner's basis. The bottom line is that if you inherit property and later sell it, you pay capital gains tax based only on the value of the property as of the date of death.

If you sell an inherited home for less than its stepped-up basis, you have a capital loss that can be deducted assuming you do not use the home as your personal residence.

However, only $3,000 of such losses can be deducted against your ordinary income per year. Any excess must be carried over to future years to be deducted.

When you inherit property, such as a house or stocks, the property is usually worth more than it was when the original owner purchased it.

If you were to sell to property, there could be huge capital gains taxes. Fortunately, when you inherit property, the property's tax basis is stepped-up, which means the basis would be the current value of the property.

For instance, if you inherit a house that was purchased several years ago for $100,000 and it is now worth $300,000. You will receive a step=up from the original cost basis from $100,000 to $300,000.

If you sell the property right away, you will not owe any capital gains taxes.

If you hold on to the property and sell it for $450,000 in a few years, you will owe capital gains on $150,000 which is the difference between the sale value and the stepped-up basis.

The only way to avoid the taxes is for you to live in the house for at least two years before selling it. In that case, you can exclude up to $250,000 or $500,000 for n couple of your capital gains from taxes.

Inheriting a house can cost the heirs money. Heirs may have to pay a variety of state and federal taxes, which may be due immediately or if they sell the property later.

The government exempts some property from taxes and offers ways to reduce taxes, depending on the heir's circumstance. In some cases, owner who inherit property and later sell it may be able to claim a tax loss.

Although the federal government suspended the estate tax for 2010, it is scheduled to return in 2011 for estates worth over $1 million. Taxes on estates worth that much including real estate, stocks, and bank accounts will be paid by the estate, rather than the heirs.

Several states levy estate taxes of their own, though others, such as California, do not. Beneficiaries pay federal inheritance tax on the net worth of their inheritance.

The net worth is the gross value less certain deductions, for instance a mortgage that must be paid off on an inherited house or a marital deduction for property inherited by a spouse.

If the result was more than the IRS exempt amount for a given year, for instance $1.45 million in 2009, the heir must pay an inheritance tax at the federal income tax rate for the non-exempt amount.

Heirs may have to pay property taxes as soon as they inherit real estate, and they will continue to pay them for as long as they own the house. Many states cap how much the assessed property value can rise from year to year, but when someone buys or inherits real estate, it will be reassessed at current market value.

Even if subsequent assessments are capped, the initial reassessment can result in heirs paying thousands of dollars more in taxes than the previous owner. Some states offer an exemption.

California state law, for instance, says that if the heir is the spouse or child of the owner, there is no reassessment. When heirs sell an inherited house, they have to pay capital gains tax on the profits.

The usual process for calculating capital gains is to subtract the market value of the home at the time it was inherited from the sale value. The heir can deduct costs such as the agent's commission from the sale amount. if the adjusted value is less than the house was worth when it was inherited, the heir may be able to claim a tax loss.

Your basis for inherited property is usually the property's value on the date of death for the person who bequeathed it to you. However, if the personal representative of the estate chose to use an alternative valuation date, your basis is the property value on that date.

The value of property, such as stocks or mutual funds, is the market price. For other types of property, the value is listed on the federal estate tax return or state inheritance tax schedule.

An inherited asset you sell for more than the basis is taxed as a capital gain, including investments and personal property. taxable gains occur from selling stocks and bonds, as well as collections like stamps and coins. Even household furnishings are subject to capital gains tax.

Selling business property that you depreciated for tax purposes after inheritance, triggers ordinary income tax, along with capital gains tax. Do not report the loss from selling any personal property, such as household goods or an automobile.

Losses on these types of property are not deductible against gains from selling other property. you also do not deduct the loss from the sale of a house, unless you rented it. No deduction is granted for a loss from the sale of a house used as your personal residence.

They say where there is a will, there is a way. And if the will names you as the sole or partial beneficiary of a home upon the death of a relative or friend, you will need to adequately prepare for the financial and personal ramifications.

Being named as a beneficiary of real estate in a will can present challenges as well as rewards. Unless you are the serving spouse, in which case legal transfer of the property to you should occur relatively quickly, seamlessly and without tax penalties, receiving an inheritance can be a long and complicated process.

It could take several weeks for the executor of the estate and the courts to divide the deceased's assets and property up, including the home.

Following the death, the executor will file the deceased's will in probate court, where a judge will determine the validity of the will. If it is considered valued, all property and assets are distributed according to the terms of the will.

Once ownership of the home is transferred to you, the government may deduct federal, state, and/or local taxes from the estate if its taxable net worth is more than a certain amount.

Inheritance tax is imposed on the transfer of assets, including real estate, at death. The rate depends on the relationship between the descendent and the inheritor.

Estate taxes, meanwhile, are imposed on the value of the property at death. The Federal government currently has an estate tax on estates worth more than $2 million dollars. Some states have an estate tax, some have an inheritance tax, and some, like Maryland, have both.

To further understand the difference between the two, an inheritance tax is an assessment made on the portion of an estate received by an individual. Eleven states still collect an inheritance tax including Connecticut, Indiana, Iowa, Kansas, Kentucky, Maryland, Nebraska, New Jersey, Oregon, Pennsylvania, and Tennessee.

An inheritance tax is different from an estate tax, which is a tax levied on an entire estate before it is distributed to individuals. If you were to inherit a home worth, say $3 million, the federal estate tax would be $450,000. If you decide to sell the inherited home, you will probably be required to pay capital gains tax on the difference between what you net from the sale and your basis, which is the purchase price plus improvements minus depreciation.

Currently, the federal capital gains tax is 15%. if the property is a personal residence and you meetcertain guidelines, you can be exempted from capital gain tax on the first $250,000 if single or $500,000 if married.

Inherited property is taxed on the value of the property the day the owner died. It is easier to sell the home after death because you get a new basis, the value on the date of death, and, therefore, less capital gains tax.

However, some end up having to sell the home to pay the estate taxes due. If it is one parcel of land worth $10 million, for instance, and there are no others assets, then you may have to sell the land in get cash to pay the $3.6 million in federal estate taxes, due within nine months of death.

After a property is inherited, it should be appraised to determine its fair market value at the time of death.

This is meant to establish a new tax basis for the property if it is eventually sold. If you have decided to sell the inherited home, you will need to determine a price and terms to sell the property.

Your will also likely hire hire a real estate broker as well as various consultants, including an appraiser, surveyor, real estate lawyer, accountant, and environmental consultant.

A mistake people often make is that a family member offers another relative $5 million for the property, and the relative turns the offer down, so it has to be worth more than that.

When someone is not willing to sell a property, a buyer may throw out a ridiculous number in a conversation, but that does not mean it is worth that or would sell for that. you have to value property based on deals that have closed or actual value.

CHAPTER 10
PREPPING AN OLD HOME TO SELL

Getting the Smell Out

Y ou need to check for any orders. Ask a friend for or neighbor to help you because they will be able to small orders you are used to and therefore do not notice any more. Obviously you want the home you inherited to look and smell as new, clean and fresh as it possibly can.

More often than not, the bad smell is caused by mold, mildew, and the releasing of foul gasses inside the house. lack of air circulation further enhances these problems, If the house is not lit properly, more complications can he expected.

First and foremost, try finding out the source of the moisture and take actions to remove the problem. you may also need to call professional if there is cracked foundation, water leak or roof leakage. It becomes really easy to fix the problem once you have found the source.

Using a dehumidifier to keep the moisture level down in a place that stays damp and dark is also a good idea. If you can dry the area, it would be beneficial.

Scrubbing the smelly areas of the house by using boric acid, white vinegar, and hydrogen peroxide etc. is a good way to get rid of the smell.

Once done, don't forget to ventilate the rooms with fans, open windows or keeping the air conditioning on.

Opening the windows and letting the sun shine in will also help in reducing the smell of these musty areas.

Using Zeolite powder is also an effective way some people use to deodorize the smells in the house. It is reusable and lasts a long time Charcoal is another substance that can be used to deodorize.

Baking soda is yet another safe and effective way to combat musty odors in the house. you can do it by spraying baking soda over the problem area, which will help in waking up any moisture and defuse the smell, It is preferable to leave or overnight and then vacuum up in the morning.

Repairs to Consider

When selling a home that you have inherited, your rooms will look larger if the walls are light colored and the lighting is bright. If any walls are painted in a dark color, you might want to think about painting them white or off-white.

If the walls are a light color, but dirty, another coat should freshen them up. Increasing the wattage of the light bulbs in the house can really brighten it up, too. If your house is carpeted, you should replace any overly stained or odorous areas.

If you don't want to replace the carpet, a good shampooing should take out the worst of the dirt and make it smell better. Clean and polish all the mirrors and windows.

You should also thoroughly clean your oven and stove. Clean the drip pans under each burner and the over, Ensure all the dirt build-up and grease are removed.

Polish the exterior of the oven and stove until it shines. you also need to clean the other appliances such as the dishwasher and refrigerator. Clean all the kitchen countertops and try to have them uncluttered. Try to reduce the number of items in all the cabinets in the house, including the kitchen cabinets.

Clean the window treatments, including blinds, and get rid of all the fingerprints around the light switches and door knocks. Be sure the areas around the trash cans are cleaned. especially the one in the kitchen.

Make sure the clothes in your closets are hanging nearly, rather than being overcrowded. Remove some of the items on the floor and shelves, so the room look clear and more specious. Your basement garage and attic space should also be cleaned and tidied up.

If the home you inherited has any sequences, leaks or rattles, do everything you can to eliminate them. These raises and sounds can give the impression there is a lot of work which needs to be done. Tighten any loose screws, bolts or nuts on doorknobs, light switches and cabinet hinges.

Tack down any loose moldings. You might want to clean and replace the caulking in the house. if your steps, stairs or banister are loose, tighten them up. Repair any water leaks and get rid of any signs of water damage. You can paint over the water stains or replace damaged wallpaper. Fix any doors or windows that do not open and close smoothly.

Selling your home requires you to pay attention to a bunch of different things. In addition to talking about the financial details to agents, you need to keep your house in the best condition possible for selling.

Every buyer who tours your house is going to be looking for something a little bit different, but you can do a few things to help make your house as appealing as possible to everybody. Every home takes an the personality of the person who owns the house. This is going to happen normally.

However, if you are ready to put your house up for sale, you need to hide as many of your personal items as you possibly can.

This means that you need in put all of your family photos out of sight. It also includes other personal items that may be on the walls or counters, such as certificates, posters, trophies and so forth.

The reason that you do this is because you want all of you potential buyers to see your home as their next home.

If you have items from your personal life all over the place, this is difficult for buyers to do. So even though you love your mementos, your decorations and your photos, it is better to keep them hidden when you have people coming to look at your house.

Painting the outside of your home might be a little expensive, but it may be an excellent way to convince potential buyer to pick your house. It may be worthwhile to have this done, especially if the house is overdue for a paint job, If your whole house does not need to be painted a touch up might be all that is necessary.

You should paint the exterior of your home and your door while you're at it. this is what visitors will see when they initially come in Another things you should paint is your mailbox, especially if it badly needs to be painted.

Other exterior features like your fence or garage door should be painted as well.

Before someone buys a house, they usually get It professionally inspected. You might want to do this yourself, get your home inspected if you want it to sell. You may not be aware of certain problems that only an inspector can locate.

The inspector is useful in that they can tell you what repairs should be done prior to the sale. Before the sale of the house, the inspector can tell you if there is roof damage, or perhaps if you have termites that need to be taking care of. It is in your best interest to fix any repair that must be done prior in the sale, instead of being surprised at a paint in the future.

You need to take an honest look at your entire home when preparing it for sale. Fixing anything that is broken, and cleaning up your home inside and out, is absolutely necessary.

Using strategies and tips listed here, you should be able to get your homes looking its best in no time at all. From top to bottom, your home needs to be cleaned and repaired.

Just use our recommendation, and any others you can think of, to make it sell as quickly as possible.

Tips to Those Who Want to Sell anInherited Home

Tip #1:

The price of the property is very important for both the owners of the property and the buyers. If it is period at a higher price than the market value, then it can be difficult to sell first. If it is priced at a lower price than the market value, then the owner will not profit from the deal.

Three tips to determine an ideal price of the property are listed as below:

- An easy way in find the correct price of the home for sale is in pretend as if you want to buy a home in your area and inquire about its pricing.

To be more precise, try and visit a property for sale that is very similar to your property for sale.

- Alternatively, you can visit a local real estate office.

They have a list of similar properties in the area and can tell you the most appropriate price of your property.

In some case, they can also help sell the home for you.

- An effective way to quickly sell in this economic down-market is to offer a partial financing option.

There are thousands of buyers in the market who have the ability to pay loan installments, but are considered ineligible by the banks.

The concept of preparing the home for sale is a concept based on the very famous marketing concept which is, "that what locals good sells really fast".

For staging a home in the best way, it is important that you port yourself in the buyer's house and imagine how they will respond to your property. They tips related to preparing the home for sale at the learnt price are listed as below:

Clean the Outside of the House: The outside of the house in the first thing that the prospective buyer will notice about the property.

You can clean it by picking up all the garbage thrown, mow the grass, remove dry leaves and grows and use a wooden broom to sweep it.

- Consider Minor Repairs: Have a thorough look at the home for sale and check which parts of it need repairs.

Pay close attention to the tape, showers, toilet seats, kitchen sink, washing machine connections, electric boards, and switches.

Although these are very minor things, they may signal issues for the prospective buyer if not in good condition. Therefore, consider repairing them.

- Empty the Home for Sale as Much as Possible: An empty home looks more specious and much bigger.

While doing the, ensure that your personal belongingness are not out in the open inside the home for sale.

Be Aware of the Three Major Causes of Seller's Stress:

Selling your home is never easy. you are emotionally attached. Not necessarily in the home itself, but to the memories that look place in it.

To minimize stress, it is best to work with an experienced seller's agent. A real agent that is used to working with homeowners looking to sell has experience in the process and understands the needs of the seller.

This all benefits you as the seller. The three highest areas of stress when selling you home includes the appraisal process, home inspections, and showing and open houses.

Be Prepared to Repair

Instead of waiting until your home is days away from being listed for sale, take time to repair the things in your home that are not suitable in buyers. This process can take anywhere from six to nine months.

Preparing ahead of time allows you to hire a reputable handyman to come in and service the areas within the home that need to be fixed before your home goes on the market. Waiting until the last minute only causes more stress and tension between you and the person making the repairs.

Compile a list of things that need to be done and within what time frame in order to minimize downtime.

Make note of all of the recent updates for home buyers to access when looking into purchasing your time. You can even go ahead and take an estimate of the coasts that are involved in the repairs and plan accordingly.

Prepare to Be Fair

Having your home appraised is one of the most difficult events in selling a home. Not every repair that was done on home will recoup its value in the asking price of your homes. Some repairs or upgrades done to the home will only be for you and will not cause in increase in the asking price.

Being prepared for appraisal process will alleviate a great deal of stress for you as the seller. The memories you made in the home are not valuable to anymore else. The home is being valued on what it is in comparison to other homes available on the market wish similar offerings.

That is it. The process should now be taken personally as that will only add stress.

Prepare Your Home

Preparing your home for sale is one of the most cleaning experiences and should be thought of as just that. Take the stress out of preparing by organizing and criminating unnecessary furniture and clutter.

Create a routine that allows you to prepare your blame for showing without really doing anything out of the ordinary new normal routine. In the morning before you leave for the day, take time to make bodes, put dishes in the dishwasher and do one complete loads of laundry.

Then you will be in the evening when the agent schedules a viewing or if someone wants to see your house during the day. Minor preparations, spending ten in fifteen minutes in the morning and at night can keep you from being stressed during unexpected showings.

Keep All Things in Perspective

Don't worry if the house doesn't smell like freshly looked goods or if pillows aren't all perfectly fluffed.

Buyers that are really interested in buying your home are not gonna take those things into account as much as they will that the house looks well-kept and is clutter-free.

Preventing Theft and Vandalism

Theft and vandalism are quite common things for unoccupied properties. If not properly taken care, it could be real turn off during the selling process, and more so that it can be a cause of good amount of money.

There are a few things that you need to keep in mind to minimize the chances. They key point is that you should not make it obvious and glaring that the house is unoccupied and that it does not have any kind of monitoring.

This will encourage criminals to damage or rob the property. You can use various methods in order to make sure that you have a propter monitoring system on the house.

- To avoid theft and vandalism, It is very important that you keep the property property lit. Keeping the exterior lights on in the front, back, and sides of the house is considered a good strategy.

This will help ward off vandalism and theft quite effectively.

- Try covering the windows properly.

Don't use newspapers as it clearly shows that the house is actually vacant.

- If you can. parking a space car in the driveway will be a huge indicator that the house is occupied.

- Try keeping the landscape in a good shape.

Use lawnmowers and if you can maintain flower beds, it would be nice.

- Know to your neighbors.

You may even consider exchanging your phone number and encourage them to call you if they see something suspicious.

- Using an alarm system on the property is also a good way of minimizing theft and vandalism.

CHAPTER 11
TIPS

When selling an inherited home, the best process of selling the property is to always hire a real estate agent who will take quality pictures of your property. A virtual tour is essential in today's market as well. Remember that your property will be marketed on the internet. A top much visual presentation is key to attracting potential buyers.

When renovating, give attention to the the location around you. Building a pool is a great improvement at any time. Building a pool, tennis court, guest house, and spa in an area filled with single family home, however, may not be the best choice.

If you house is significantly more improved that the homes in the surrounding area, you will have trouble selling when the time comes. In spite of the fact that this is your real estate agent's job, you need to ensure that the photographs of your home look great when you selling it.

These photographs are an initial introduction for your potential buyer and you need to make sure that it presented well. Take a look at different properties and contrast your photograph style with theirs. Ensure that the photographs show an entire room and not simply pictures of furniture in a room.

You will have more enthusiasm for your property with the correct photographs. The best way for real estate agents and sellers to find new business is mailing out marketing advertisements to potential buyers.

These are individual whose property didn't sell and for some reason didn't re-sing with their prior real estate agents. So they may be in the market for another agent to work with. Market targeting and expired listing can expand their listings by 15% to 20%. Leave room to negotiated when you are setting your asking price for your home.

Buyers may not work with a seller or real estate agent who is not willing to negotiate the price, regardless of the fact that the house is accurately evaluated at fair market value. You need to appear interested and willing to negotiate.

To locate the best real estate agents to sell your property, request a rundown of the comparable homes sold in your general vicinity for as far back as year.

Look over the comparable list to check whether one organization or specialist sold more than others in your neighborhood. They will have contacts with potentials buyer for any range.

At the end of the day, selling a home does not need to be an exceptionally difficult process. If you consider and issue the tips listed, you should be able to sell your house in no time.

Here are Ten Tips to Help Marketing anAcquired Home

Tip #1: Be Objective

Purchasers are generally occupied with value, area, condition, speculation security and size.

Your sentimental memories or attachment to the home doesn't make a price difference. Try not to bring your feelings into the cost of your home.

Tip #2: Forget What Your Home Used to Be Worth

Disregard what your home used to be worth. It doesn't make a difference. Land costs change. You need to offer in today's market value.

Tip #3: Don't Anticipate Finding a Sucker

Many individuals might believe that their agent can find that one sucker who is willing pay more for their home than it is truly worth. Does it happen? Yes of course it does.

Does it happen regularly enough for you to depend on? No.

Tip #4: What Will Your Home Be Worth Later On?

Time is money if you property value is decreasing.

You will put more cash in your pocket if you offer today versus 6 months from now. The quicker you after, the better.

Tip #5: Analyze the Market

This is the place where a good real estate agent can prove to be useful.

I've worked near a few specialists who put around five-minute' worth of work into landing and asking cost. Sometimes that might work, but more often than not, it doesn't.

Take a look at the properties presently on the market, under contract, and as of late sold and expired.

many individuals neglect to take a look at the expired postings. These need to be examined to see happened to you don't commit the same errors. How does your home compare to the as of late sold properties? Once more, ensure you are being objective.

Tip #6: More Publicizing Does Not LegitimizeOverpricing

I do believe that great marketing is vital in an awful market. you need to separate yourself from the a great many different properties available to be purchased.

In any case, that does not imply that huge amounts of print publicizing, an open house each Sunday and a large number of "Just Listed" cards are going to offer an overrated home.

Incredible marketing might get a buyer in the doorway, but that same purchaser will take a look at other listings. Intensely promoting an overrated home might just offer your legitimately-valued rival a chance to sell.

Tip #7: Evaluations Are a Primary Concern

You would prefer not to experience the bother of offering your home and everything goes runs with it and discover that your home did not evaluate out.

Build up an asking price in accordance with as of late sold comparable homes and you won't have an issue.

Tip #8: Get in Front of the Market

On the off chance that your market is dropping, don't follow it down. Be proactive and get in front of it and you will put more cash in your pocket.

Tip #9: Be the Best

This is not advanced science. Buyers just need to purchase the best house at the best cost.

Know your competition very well. Stay in contact with your agent and visit comparative homes that are listed with yours. When you see those properties, it is easier to make comparisons. In a down market, your need to create a feeling of worth for purchasers.

If a buyer is uncertain about pricing falling further, they may not purchase until they feel that they getting a good value and a fair price.

Tip #10: Be Prepared to Lower Your Price

You may not get your asking price in the beginning. In some cause, this may be difficult to handle. The first asking cost is only the beginning stage. Try not to fixate on your asking price too much.

Be sure that you lower your price before your home gets stale. In the event that your home has been on the market too long, many agents will stop showing your home since they may assurance that you are not a legitimate seller.

Hopefully, you will find these tips useful. Selling an acquired home, you simply need pay attention your property's surroundings.

CHAPTER 12
HOW TO GET BUYERS BEGGINGTO VIEW YOUR HOME

Floor are a key feature buyers notice in your home. Buyers will be sure to notice how warm they are, and if the floors need to be replaced. Let's face it, floors can be quite expensive and difficult to replace.

Everyone notices flooring,should you clean or replace?

Good news is, replacing is not your only option.

Installing new floor coverings of any kind, including carpeting, hardwood or tile, can get pricey. Costs vary widely, based on the size of your rooms and the flooring material used.

Use these cleaning tips to avoid expensive flooring work.

Carpeting

Carpets take a beating. General traffic, pets, children, muddy, shoes, coffee, and wine all leave their calling cards on your carpeting. Unless you have been extremely fussy about your carpeting, it shows signs of use. This job calls for more than a good vacuum.

Shampoo: You can often rent or purchase a carpet shampooer inexpensively, If your carpet does not have stains, spruce it up with a good washing:

- ☐ Move the furniture out of the rooms you need to shampoo.
- ☐ Follow the shampooer instructions,
- ☐ Go over the carpet thoroughly to remove all soap residence.
- ☐ Keep all traffic off the carpet until it is completely dry.

You should see a significant difference in both the smell and look of your carpet. Buyers will notice the fresh, clean feeling too.

Steam Clean: Stained carpet need in depth treatment than a regular carpet shampooer can offer. If that is the cause, go with a steam cleaning and spot treatment:

- ☐ Rent a steam cleaning shampooer.
- ☐ Hire a professional carpet cleaner.

If you are dealing with severe stains or damage, get a cleaning estimate first. Then compare the price to replacing the carpet. Cleaning can make a tremendous difference, and save the cost of replacement.

Sometimes deep cleaning works, but cannot remove an extra stubborn stain. Other times there is only one bad spot. you may be able to cover up with rugs. Adding a tasteful area ur throw rug makes the room a little more attractive for showings.

Don't be dishonest about a trouble spot. If your carpet was in bad enough shape a steam cleaning did not take out all of the stains, it will be evident in buyers the carpet needs to be replaced.

Even if your carpet is beyond the help of a professional cleaning you may not want to replace it.

New carpeting is a big expense for most people to fit into their budgets. Carpet, like paint, is a very personal choice. It would be a shame to re-carpet, only to discover a family loved everything about your hose but the carpeting you just purchased!

Instead, work with what you have. Clean it and put down rugs. Keep it vacuumed. Stop people from eating and drinking on it effective immediately. Confine pets to rooms with slick floors for easy mopping. Do everything you can to keep the carpet forum getting works.

If a buyer loves everything in your home, except for the ugly carpeting, they might overlook it. They may be willing to negotiate a lower price or accept a flooring allowance in your final contract.

Obviously, a clean carpet is best. these alternative options can help you keep costs low, and still make a good impression.

Other Flooring Types

Take the same approach with other types of flooring. No matter the material, if you have a floor that is a little worse for wear, clean it thoroughly. Pay attention to special details that vary on each material.

Take tiny steps until you find the right fix. Your hardwood floor can probably get by with a good works. Vacuum the joints, where dirt accumulates, refinishing is a last resort. Give your tile floors a heavy scrubbing. Clean the great joints in between the tiles. If that doesn't work, have it re-grated.

In some instances, you might feel the only option is to replace flooring. Make this a last resort. You might be pleasantly surprised how some tender loving care can make a floor shine!

When these non-carpet flooring types need more than a cleaning, consider repairs. However, in some cause, it is cheaper in replace your floor than to have it repaired.

If your current flooring is damaged beyond repair, you may have to replace it. When you do, consider less expensive flooring options. For example, vinyl self-stick tiles are inexpensive, easy to install, and simple to replace when damaged.

Brighten up the housewith new bright light bulbs.

Lighting is an essential element to update when prepping your house for sale. Similar to flooring, buckle lighting improvements by reparsing what you can and replacing the word filatures.

The single most important key to lighting is this; be moderate and practical wish your updates.

Why? The National Agent's Association reveals many home buyers will replace lighting fixtures as one of the first changes to their new home.

With this in mind, there is no need to go overboard in spending big on lighting fixture updates. Help existing fixtures look their best.

Here's a cost saving idea to refurbish the good light fixtures you already have in place. Follow these tips to save cash:

- ☐ Use the same spray painting principles you practiced on your handles, pulls, and knobs.
- ☐ New globes give an old fixture an update look.
- ☐ If repairing an old fixture will cost more than replacing, just replace it with something tasteful, but simple.
- ☐ Replace any light fixtures that are broken, damaged. or dangerous in any way.
- ☐ Put in new light bulbs to brighten room up.
- ☐ Clean the fixtures you are not updating. Inside and out.
- ☐ Don't' forget the outside lights.

Great lighting is important when showing a home. When potential buyers walk into a bright, well-lit house, they get a feeling of openness and trust. Plus, you put in a lot of hard work cleaning. Light everything up, and let your home shine!

Bright lighting also makes an area look more open and alternative. This will make closet and rooms in your home feel larger.

One more tip: change old, haggard ceiling fan blades. Look for inexpensive ones at any hardware superstore.

Revamp the front entrance.

Take a step outside of the house and onto your front lawn. Don't feel had if you've gotten so wrapped up in updating and improving the inside of your home you have neglected the outside.

It happens to all of us.

You can certify the situation quickly and efficiently. Here is what to address first: the front entryway. The first thing to work on is the lock and knob of your front door.

Take a hard look at your doorknob. What do you see?

- ⬚ Is it a mousy little knob from decades long past?
- ⬚ Is it dented or rusted? Does the key stick? Is it hard to open?
- ⬚ Could someone break in with a bobby pin and patience?

If you answered "yes" to any of these questions, you definitely need to replace your door handle with a heavy-duty deadbolt and knob combination.

Why? The knob is the first point they touch on your home.

A flimsy lock and handle on your front door tells potential home buyers your home isn't secure. It makes them feel uncomfortable, and they won't even know why.

So, get a nice, big, sturdy set and they'll feel your home is as safe as can be.

Now take a good look at your door. Is it pleasing to look at? Or is it weathered and dinged up? Has your mental door never seen a coat of paint? Is the paint on it peeled and flaking? It is time for change.

Here are two simple ways to put a new face on your house:

- ☐ Add a dash of color. Choose paint compliments the color of your home.
- ☐ Use faux painting techniques to transform your metal door into a good grain look-alike.

If your door is severely damaged, have it fixed or replaced entirely. As always, go with whichever costs less.

You've addressed the living area inside of your home. Your front entrance is inviting. Now is the time to take a critical look at your front yard.

Curb Appeal is very important.

Curb appeal (how your home looks from the road) is the most important image of all. You want to make an amazing first impression. A well-prepared house can even catch the eyes of buyers who never intended to visit your home.

Buyers driving by who look at your home should immediately feel as though they want to go inside. This will not happen if you have poor landscaping, a dingy exterior, or an unkempt yard.

Look around your yard and list everything that needs a little work.

- ☐ Are your shrubs, trees, flower gardens, and walkways tidy?
- ☐ Is three trash or just a general mess in your yard?
- ☐ Does everything (front light, garage door, porch rails, etc.) function property, and look its best?
- ☐ Could outdoor features, like patio furniture or the garage door, be updated with a quick coat of paint?

Chances are excellent you'll have a little improving to do. Take heart: just think of how many people are going to beg to view the inside of your home when they see how beautiful it is from your curb!

This might seem like an overwhelming list, but the truth is it takes hard work to get a home ready to sell. Anyone can put a house on the market. Not everyone sells quickly or with great profits.

Thankfully, you now have a big advantage over other sellers. You know what it takes. Follow these guidelines to gain the best advantage for your home to sell quickly, and for the best price.

CHAPTER 13
IMPORTANCE OF GOOD PICTURES

You've heard it before and you'll hear it again, your main goalin selling your home is to make money. Whether this is to make a profit or to pay off your current mortgage, your focus needs to be us ranking that sale.

Not excited about the idea? You can have loads of fun with it. For starters, how are you taking pictures?

Pictures play a huge role in nailing that sale. If you have great pictures, you'll set yourself up above other homeowners handling for the same buyers. Think about it.

If you had to purchase a home in a particular city for work purposes and there were only two for sale in that city that could fit your needs, which seller would you trust more from the get-go? The one who posts casual picture that capture dishes in the sink or a sock in the corner, or the one who give the impression of a pristine lifestyle?

You can show off your pristine lifestyle and build up the buyer's confidence in the quality of your home by putting in a little extra effort isn't it true that the real winners in every category of life are ones who put out the need effort?

Need some ideas? Read through these tips to help get the ball rolling:

Pretend that you are shouting for a magazine. It all starts with cleaning, cleaning, cleaning! Get rid of the clutter. move out old and ugly furniture, and hide away all of your personal belongings.

You don't want your family photo, laundry, or the old turn lounge chair online for the world to see.

Shelter the pets. This is important, Even if you're the most meticulous pet owner in the world, advertising to potential buyers that you have birds in a cage, a free roaming guinea pig, or a bedroom dedicated to a family of rare Siamese cats is going to scare people away.

Pets often create odors that stick around for a while, and since you'll be working hard to make this odor disappear, you want to avoid bringing any attention to these critters.

Don't only hide them from the photos, find another place to shelter them if you want the most luck making the sale.

Add sprinkles on top. A few hours accessories with colors that pop will go a long way. Do you have any bright sofa pillows?

How about a healthy green plant or a vase of colorful flowers strategically placed in each room?

Light it up. Are you pictures really dark or washed out?

Not enough light from the windows? Add some lighting to bring them up a level. Bright LED lamps in the corners or off-camera can add just the retouch you need.

Hire a stager. If you don't want to go through the effort on your own, you can hire a professional stager who can come in to rearrange the furniture or even hiring in some accessories or extra pieces of furniture.

When you're interviewing different stagers for the job, make sure to check on rates per room. You may decide to only photograph certain rooms in the house, but you'll win bigger with more pictures.

Hire a photographer. Although you can take great pictures on your own without a very expensive camera, you might having a pro do the work.

This can give you an even greater advantage over other sellers by helping to increase the perceived value of your home.

Photos of the Outside

It goes without saying that your potential buyers want to see the inside and the outside in any online listing or property website that you have. If you're going to show them, show them! Before taking pictures, take these important steps:

Cut that grass. Whether you do it yourself or support your neighborhood professional, give your lawn a clean, close out.

Get rid of some tension with your weed-whacker by obliterating those stubborn weeds and extra strands of grass along pathways, the house, and around trees.

Trim the hedges. If there is one thing that helps to look like an abandoned hideout. It's a runway row of hedges.

You can save the day by a quick trim to make sure that the bushes are nice and even, adding another spark of life to the outside.

Colorful landscaping. Plant a variety of colorful flowers, and lay some red cedar chips.

If you would like to provide a night photo for effect, consider adding some LED path light.

Give it a bath. Shine the windows, hose down the house, and clean the gutters. Sweep the pathways and driveway. you don't want pictures of cobwebs around you doorways or of water-stained windows.

Take strategic photo from angels that really show off your home. Following the above tips should make this easier because you won't be trying to avoid capturing the grass or bushes in the photos

Drones

In the past, you would have needed to pay an expensive fee to a pilot for the use of a private plane or helicopter. Now, you can make it all happen more affordable with drones.

Besides being used by some to spy on neighbors, drones have a variety of uses. The good news is that one of these is to show off the high value of your home to potential buyers.

As regulation continues to shape the future of drones and their legal use by civilians, you can still stay ahead of the crowd by high licensed drone photographer or getting the license to fly one yourself,

Why does drone photography give you an advantage over other sellers?

Provides a big picture view.you can give potential buyers a complete view of your property by an aerial photograph or video.

This is something that most homeowners never see for themselves for as many ears as they have been in their homes.

The house, the yard, the distance from neighbors – this is a valuable shot.

Shows the road home. If you choose to have the drone capture video footage, you can take the potential buyers on a ride up the street to your home and even pull up into the driveway and walk them to the front door.

Whether doing it yourself or hiring an experienced professional, take sure to draw up a plan.

Map out the route, plan the time of day, and be prepared to take multiple photographs or video shots to give yourself options.

Do you want to benefits from the lighting effects of service or unset? Do you want to catch the school bus route?

Do you want to include any wildlife around your property such a deer?

Think ahead. Planning the details will help your drone project above smoothly and provide a valuable finished product.

Video Walk-Through

We're now a raile ahead of the rest. This is every home buyer'sdream.

You could use drone or use your camera, but either way, taking potential buyers on a walk through their future home could be just the activation they seed to further explore the purchase and sign the contract.

How many contracts do you have to you home? Consider starting a separate video from each door and walking through the home to give the viewers multiple perspectives.

The more you can give, the more value you will create, the more offers you will receive, and the more quickly you will make the sale.

To take it up another notch, consider making it a guided tour by either having someone walk in front of the camera while explaining each room, or make it a guided tour with a voice-over.

There's always someone in your circle who has a great voice, so if it's not you, ask this person for a favor. Otherwise, you can hire voice-over professional through on online agency.

If you could save a few long-distance potential buyers the cost of a plane trip, you've already want in their eyes. It now gives them a sense of urgency to be the first to snatch up your house before it's gone.

CHAPTER 14
REPAIRS OR TOUCH-UPS TO IMPROVE VALUEHOME IMPROVEMENTS THAT INCREASE YOUR HOME'S VALUE

First of all, keep in mind that you don't need a giant improvement to achieve your goal. Small improvements introduced in almost every room, including the exterior of the house is what we are aiming for.

Here are some tips to get your started:

☐ Clean, Clean and Clean. Nothing looks more appealing and eye-catching than a neat and clean house. So, start improving the appearance of your house by cleaning out the debris, making your garden look like an ideal place and painting or polishing the front door to make it more welcoming.

Decluttering is also a part of cleaning. So, get rid of things you don't need to make room for new ones.

☐ The first glance is usually is enough to tell a lot about a house.

Go out and see how other people would judge your exterior.

Does it need repainting? Is there a walkway that you can highlight by introducing some flowers?

Keep it simple but try to make it neat.

That is what we look for when we are inspecting houses to buy one.

▢   The kitchen usually needs an upgrade whether it has been used or is still new and untouched.

Renovating it using modern decor is going to instantly improve the value of your home.

Why ?

Because people have an eye for the kitchen and they want it to be just perfect.

Even if they would have to compromise on other rooms, they will buy a home just because it's kitchen is well maintained and inviting.

▢   Other than kitchen, bathrooms are something people usually inspect very closely.

Replace the faucets, and clean up the bathroom counter. We would again emphasize on simplicity because simple and neat arrangements are usually easy to clean and maintain.

What to invest in?

So, you're done decluttering, cleaning and upgrading.

What's next ? Well, if you have a good investment to make for your home, it is recommended to divided it into three or four parts to bring some really impressive improvements to your home.

Here are some areas you might want to think about seriously.

Lighting: If you are not very satisfied with the lighting system in your home, replace it.

But for this you would need to buy fixtures and other equipment for each and every room in order to make it look consistent and attractive.

Plumbing: Many old homes have rusty pipes and even some leakage in the plumbing that needs serious attention.

Your home will not sell fast and at a price you have in mind if you haven't already invested in making the plumbing system better and improved.

Flooring: Most people nowadays look for hand wood floors or alternatives that are easy to manage and provide health benefits instead of carpeting.

Tiled floors are also fairly acceptable. If you think this improvement would bring you high profits, make it right away.

HVAC Replacement: With the passage of time, new and more energy-efficient systems are being introduced to the market that incur a one time cost and help you save huge amounts of money on utility bills. If you want to add a new and unique selling point to your ad, make this replacement as part of your home improvement strategy and see how offers start coming.

What's really worth repairing?

Remember that it is not wise to spend your money on each and everything just to have it repaired. Not all things are worth repairing, some need to be thrown out and others need to be replaced. This is one principle that most people follow when they stage their home.

Inspect each and every aspect of your home and then come up with a plan that will go with your budget and also bring improvement to your home. You may want to replace outdated appliances in the kitchen. Repairing these machines is not an option. So you will have to get rid of them and buy new ones.

If your budget doesn't allow this upgrade, simply give the ones you use a color-boost or something like that to at least improve their appearance.

If you already have wooden floors installed at home, look for scratches and be prepared for some refinishing. This is one aspect most home buyers would look into closely, but there's no need to replace the entire flooring.

Wooden floors look great even if they are old and worn out. Give them a little lift-up to make them more attractive and appealing.

Nowadays energy efficiency has found its way into many of our system including the windows. Now people look for the latest windows and other systems that are designed to be more energy efficient providing a number of health and environmental benefits.

Replace your old windows for these new ones if you want to improve the value of your home through small yet significant changes.

If your bathroom floors are tiled, look for flaws or cracks especially if the tiles are white or light colored. These types of flaws are hard to conceal even if you arrange everything else very neatly.

So, before investing in other bathrooms accessories and putting in your efforts to de-clutter it, replace a cracked floor tile.

CHAPTER 15
SELLING PROCESS FOR AN INHERITED HOME

H aving to deal with the passing of a loved one, especially a mother or father can be process that can take week or months.

Whether your mother or Father's death was unpredicted or not, you need to handle the stress in dealing with your family inheritance. Seeing your name on the inheritance list to inherit your house, you can choose to either keep the real estate in the family name or sell it off during a normal home sale transaction.

Here are the guidelines that will assist you to go through the transaction if you want to sell a home which has been inherited.

Verify the title status of the house

The whole process of selling an inherited piece of real estate is quite difficult, and the first step is usually to verify that your deceased loved one was actually the property owner.

Hire a real estate lawyer and let them check the status of the house. Allow them to verify if your deceased parent's) or guardian's) was the owner of the house you would like to sell.

Probate Court and Creditors

If you have confirmed that the legal owner of the property was your parent, then it may need to pass through probate court, depending on its value.

A legal court will likely demand one of the heirs to acquire a license to sell a house in your state. You will need to double check if this is a requirement.

The next step you must do is the Creditor's Claims Process

If there are any outstanding debts incurred by the deceased person's, debt collectors will be able to claim what owed to them from the inheritance.

All assets of the same procedure before they can be given to the heirs.

Investigate the Market

The next thing is to review the market. Examine and record the listing and selling prices for comparable homes in your neighbourhood. You may need repair the parts of the home that need to be fixed.

If you want to sell your home quickly, list the property below the market price. If you home is in bad condition, make an effort to sell it to investors rather than mainstream buyers.

Talk with Bidders and make the Sale

The final step is to talk to possible real estate buyers. To be able to sell a property quickly, everyone should be flexible with the cost if the buyers asks for a lower price.

Having said that, you should have the minimum cost of the house set.

Emotions run higher when it comes to selling real estate that was included as part of an inheritance. So you need to be carefully advised about the worth of liquidating your loved one's assets as a way of putting the death behind you.

Most people know that when you inherit a house, it can often be a bittersweet experience in several ways.

We may be mourning the loved one who has passed away, and is addition we start mourning our own sanity in the midst of family fights. Many disagreements can come up on the topic of how to sell a house.

It seems that everybody has his or her own opinion, and that goes double when times tough. These days, economic times are stressful enough without adding more stress into the mix. However, after a death when a house must be sold, the process can generate even more stress for everyone in this difficult time.

At the risk of sounding rather morbid, the very best time to think about how to sell a house is before it becomes necessary to do so.

Although it's not pleasant to think about, giving serious consideration to your sale long before you inherit a house can set the course to move forward whenever the time arrives.

But sometimes other siblings can become very uncooperative in the process because they are offended by the idea of planning ahead for someone's death, even though it makes sense and show mature, responsible asset management.

Sometimes our own relatives don't agree about what needs to be done and when it needs to be done when selling your home. Nobody should try to tell you what to do regarding your own family, but I say one thing for certain. Be sure to prepare in advance prepared and just keep your preparations to yourself if need be. Leave your brothers and sisters out of the loop of information you are gathering, especially if you expect them to have issues with your plans.

Take notes when you speak with lawyers and other professionals, getting their advice and suggestions for a month sale when there are related sellers.

Now, this next suggestion may surprise you, but there is one thing I definitely would avoid doing. I would avoid speaking to a real estate agent in advance because that is guaranteed to get your siblings and/or their spouses on the offence.

If you're expecting any disagreements, this may trigger them, which was my experience when I needed to sell my house.

I've taken note that most people have friends and, of course, we all have our own sphere of influence, so we know real estate agents and consider them to be friends. Since most of us want to do business with people we know, this will apply to our siblings as well.

This is a particular situation that can cause a disagreement when it's time to put an inherited house on the market because each heir will want to work with people they know personally in order to sell a house.

Once you've got your inherited house, you may be thinking of selling or keeping it. If your next plan is to sell it, the thing you may want to inquire is, how can I sell my home quickly?

With foreclosure, repossession and more properties on the real estate market, the entire process of marketing your house may take some time. The following are the choices you'll be able to take in order to sell your property quickly.

Sell your Property On Your Own

The option to sell a house yourself could save cash that wouldotherwise pay an agent. However, prepare yourself for the challenges that will arise. You must work on successions, appraisals, placing, ads, open house, along with property stinging and repairs. You'll need flexible time to manage all these duties, finished in a suitable and timely manner to sell the home.

Selling with Real Estate Professional

For those who have good enough budget, it is a great idea to hire an agent. This would help you avoid any possible stress from selling your house. They will do all the process required in selling the property like setting the prices of the prices of the house, marketing, home showing, organizing selling and closing process. And the great advantage is, your home has much more exposure to the real estate market.

Real Estate Investor

Hiring a real estate investor is a way of getting a fast sale on the home. It's not necessary to worry about paying a commission. They're going to buy your home no matter what its present condition. No maintenance tasks needed.

Auction

In addition in the real estate investor, you can find another way to sell your house quickly. No more maintenance required since it will be bought as it is.

Understanding how to sell your home fast is a good idea because it can help you stay away from fees such as the maintenance of your home, as well as, paying taxes and insurance if your house remains on market for a longer time.

Ending Thoughts

Thank you for taking the time to read this book. I hope it has helped you understand the "ins and outs" of selling an inherited home. I am more than happy to provide you with a Comparative Market Analysis and serve as your listing agent.

www.ingramcontent.com/pod-product-compliance
Lightning Source LLC
Chambersburg PA
CBHW070352220526
45467CB00001B/353